HOW TO REACH
BABY BOOMERS

EFFECTIVE
CHURCH
SERIES

WILLIAM EASUM

Edited by HERB MILLER

HOW TO REACH
BABY BOOMERS

ABINGDON PRESS

Nashville

HOW TO REACH BABY BOOMERS

Copyright © 1991 by Abingdon Press

Third Printing 1992

This book is printed on recycled, acid-free paper.

Library of Congress Cataloging-in-Publication Data

EASUM, WILLIAM M., 1939-
  How to reach baby boomers / William M. Easum.
    p.   cm. — (Effective church series)
  Includes bibliographical references.
  ISBN 0-687-17928-9 (alk. paper)
    1. Church work with the baby boom generation.   I. Title.
II. Series.
BV4446.E2   1991
259'.084'4—dc20   91-14244
                                                            CIP

Scripture quotations are from the Revised Standard Version of the Bible, copyright 1946, 1952, 1971, 1973 by the Division of Christian Education of the National Council of Churches of Christ in the USA. Used by permission.

MANUFACTURED IN THE UNITED STATES OF AMERICA

To my wife, Jan, and the membership of Colonial Hills Church, who have unselfishly provided me the time to travel, read, and consult with churches all across the United States. In addition, the paid staff of Colonial Hills Church has gone beyond the call of duty to fill the leadership and pastoral gaps caused by my regular absence. As a result, everyone has benefited: my understanding of human nature, and delegation skills have grown; Colonial Hills has continued to grow and venture into new ministries; the lessons learned are giving new hope to hundreds of churches in several mainstream denominations; and Jan and I have a freedom we never knew before. The Bible remains true: "Whoever loses his life for my sake will find it" (Matthew 16:25*b*).

CONTENTS

HOW TO REACH
BABY BOOMERS

FOREWORD

In the movie *Havana*, Robert Redford plays the role of a high stakes gambler, Jack Weil, who roams the casinos of the world. When a Cuban revolutionary leader asks Jack Weil why he is in Havana, Jack replies, "I came here to play cards."

"That sounds like gambling," the man says.

"I try to keep the gambling to a minimum," Jack replies.

"How do you do that?" the man asks.

"By being good at it," Jack says.

How do we keep the gambling to a minimum when we attempt to involve in our church large numbers of young and mid-life adults? By being good at it! The principles and methods Bill Easum lays out help us to achieve that goal as we reach out to that one-third of the population sociologists have labeled Baby Boomers. Others have accurately described the thinking and behavior characteristics of these seventy-six million people, but Easum makes a unique contribution. He illustrates in concrete, practical ways the numerous changes congregations must make in order to influence persons in this age bracket to make a life-changing connection with Jesus Christ and to grow spiritually in that relationship.

Easum's insights fit the goal of the Effective Church Series: to help meet the need for "how to" answers in specific areas of church life. Each of these volumes provides clergy and lay persons with practical insights and methods that can increase their congregations' effectiveness in achieving God's purposes in every aspect of ministry: leadership, worship, Sunday school, membership care, biblical literacy, spiritual growth, small groups, evangelism, new-member assimilation, prayer, youth work, singles work, young adult work, time management, stewardship, administration, community service, world mission, conflict resolution, and writing skills.

Easum's insights also fit the theological focus of the Effective Church Series. While concentrating more on the practical "how to do it" than on the theoretical and conceptual, the "ideas that work" in the Effective Church Series rest on biblical principles. Without that foundation, method sharing feeds us a diet of cotton candy, sweet but devoid of nutrients. Easum has addressed the subject of how to attract and involve Baby Boomers in ways consistent with biblical truths and classic Christian theology.

In ancient Egypt, a group of slaves was attempting to raise an obelisk onto its base. The supervising engineer watched them straining at the ropes, trying to raise the mass of granite to its intended place on the giant pedestal. They got the stone within a few inches of the goal but could get it no higher. The engineer was scratching his head, when a sailor in the group shouted out the solution to the dilemma. "Wet the ropes!" he said. They did, while everyone watched in amazement. As the ropes began to groan, strain, and shrink, the huge rock rose the final inches. Soon, the slaves were able to push it over, and the great work was completed.

Everything effective church leaders do has two background elements—the obvious mechanics that everyone knows, and the secrets that are obvious after someone with unique information points them out. In the numerous areas of church life essential to reaching Baby Boomer young adults, Easum has said in dozens of different ways, "Wet the ropes!"

Herb Miller
Lubbock, Texas

PREFACE

When I was a young man in college, two goals for my life crystallized. One was to obtain a doctor's degree in theology and the other was to write a best-selling book. By the mid 1970s it became clear that my first goal would never be reached, so I concentrated on the second goal.

My first attempt at writing in 1967 was turned down by several publishers. So I quit writing and concluded that I would never reach either of my life goals.

Then I met Kennon Callahan who encouraged me to write about my experiences as pastor of Colonial Hills Church, and as a consultant to many other churches. I did, and this time the book, *The Church Growth Handbook*, was a huge success.

But then reality set in. As someone said, "There is one good book in everyone." That statement encouraged me to try a second book. To my surprise, a second book quickly fell into place. This second book, *How to Reach Baby Boomers*, is the dream of a lifetime.

Reaching this goal would have been impossible without the encouragement of Kennon Callahan, the love and support of my wife Jan, the faithfulness of the congregation of Colonial Hills Church, and the courage of one of the finest church staffs in the world. I thank God every day for each of them.

What about your goals for your life? Have you given up on them? Perhaps you should not, at least not yet. Perhaps someone will come along to encourage you to press on or to start over. Maybe that will happen to you while reading this book.

John 14:12 reminds us that we will do greater things than Jesus did. Within each of us there is a story waiting to be told; marvelous acts waiting to be done; tremendous gifts waiting to be shared. Go. Tell. Do, and share! That is the gospel and the real purpose for all our lives.

Bill Easum
Port Aransas, Texas
March 1991

INTRODUCTION: FAST FORWARD

We have not only lost the power to coerce, but the ability to persuade people to even listen to us.
Dorothy C. Bass

How can mainstream Protestant churches prepare themselves to minister to the diverse spiritual needs of the Baby Boomer (people born between 1946–1964)? How can mainstream Protestant churches bring these young adults into a redemptive relationship with Jesus Christ? How can church leaders adapt to the vast changes that are occurring in our world? What changes are necessary if mainstream Protestant churches are to be a viable witness to Jesus Christ in the twenty-first century? This book attempts to answer these questions. Three words provide the framework for the answers—change, diversity, and choice.

A World of Change

The last twenty-five years have brought more basic changes in the life-styles and needs of people than any other period in our nation's history. Of all the changes affecting the ministry of mainstream churches, none is more important than the relationship between the church and culture. The marriage between American culture and Christianity is coming to an end. What was once a separation, is becoming a divorce. Not only is the marriage dissolving, but there are signs of actual hostility between the church and society. We are the first generation of Americans to live in an unchurched culture. People no longer attend church unless they are shown why they should attend.

A World of Diversity

Prior to World War II churches could function as if there were basically two categories of people—those who went to church and those who did not. That is no longer true. Today's world contains a wide diversity of people. Growing churches minister to at least six basic categories of people. While the members of these groups share several behavioral and thought patterns, the six categories are distinctively different from each other. Trying to lead a church without knowing these differences is like driving a car with a windshield coated with ice.

1. The thirty and under crowd is shaped by television, broken homes, and the two-wage-earner family. They are ambitious, materialistic, and skeptical. Many of them either still live at home or have in the recent past. Their driving passion is to be accepted.

2. Thirty to thirty-nine year olds were influenced by Vietnam, Woodstock, and affluence. Although commitment is not in their vocabulary, they are compassionate and emotionally responsive to life. Their driving passions are self-fulfillment and family safety.

3. The forty to forty-seven group is displaced either by upward mobility or the crunch of a changing marketplace. Their driving passion is job security or career success.

4. The forty-eight to fifty-five group is characterized as eclectic and puzzled. They have heard about the Depression and World War II, lived through Vietnam and Woodstock, and witnessed enormous technological changes. Many look back on their childhood and wish they had shown more emotion, freedom, and spontaneity when they were younger. Their driving passion is financial security.

5. People age fifty-six and older lived through one or two world wars and an economic depression. Security is of the utmost importance. Their driving passion is a commitment to duty and financial stability.

6. This final group includes people of all ages who have submitted their lives to Jesus Christ and have experienced the power of living lives on behalf of others. They have found acceptance and safety in the love of God. They have learned that self-denial is the point at which the abundant life begins. They find their security in God's love. Money is a gift to be used for others, rather than a goal of one's life. The Cross shapes this group's life.

All six groups are searching for ways to make their lives more meaningful. The groups in the forty-seven and under age range are preoccupied with getting more out of life than they are getting at the moment. Members of the forty-eight to fifty-five group wish they could relive their childhood and experience the emotion and free spirit they see exhibited in the younger crowd. This time they would not feel guilty for the children in China if they did not clean their plates. The fifty-six and older folks either look nostalgically at the past and wish to return to the good old days, or they passionately look for ways to keep life from narrowing and constricting any further as they discover ways to live their remaining years with meaning and dignity. The Cross crowd searches for new and relevant ways to live life on behalf of others.

This book concentrates on how mainstream churches can reach out to the groups forty-seven years of age and under and move them from a life preoccupied with one form or another of self-fulfillment to a life lived on behalf of others.

A World of Choices

My father bought a new car in 1947. He was so proud of the car because it was different from most other cars. His car was dark blue instead of black. Not only that, it was a convertible! My father's car was the talk of the neighborhood. The neighbors marveled that my father had the choice of buying a dark blue convertible instead of a black sedan.

People over fifty years of age read about my father's car and smile; they remember those days. But young adults read this story with a critical eye. They note the fact that the car was my "father's" car, instead of my "parents'" car. They find no excitement in my father's ability to choose the color of a car, much less a dark blue one. And they find it interesting and quaint that I used such an archaic word as neighborhood. The world has radically changed since my father bought his dark blue convertible. It is now a changing, diverse world of choice. It was not that way for my father.

What This Book Is About

This book is not about a diverse, changing world of choices; neither is it an attempt to describe the Baby Boomer in detail. Those two issues were discussed superbly in Tex Sample's book *U.S. Lifestyles and Mainline Churches,*[1] and *100 Predictions for the Baby Boom,* by Cheryl Russell.[2] Rather, this book focuses on how mainstream churches can address the diverse needs of young adults in ways that encourage them to connect with Jesus Christ.

The theme—*In order to minister to this diverse, changing world of choices, mainstream Protestant churches need to make basic changes in leadership skills, the quality and scope of ministry, and the method of preaching and worship.* Churches can accomplish these changes without abandoning any of the basic tenets of Christianity as defined by the various denominations. Nor do these changes dilute the basic substance of Christianity. But these changes do significantly alter the manner in which pastors and laity proclaim, package, market, and give leadership to the Good News.

The goal—*Everything discussed in this book is designed to move Baby Boomers from the pursuit of self-centered self-fulfillment to the biblical understanding of self-fulfillment through self-denial.* Baby Boomers find the abundant life they seek only on the other side of the cross of Jesus Christ.

Expect Tension

Be forewarned. Responding to the needs of Baby Boomers may create some tension in your life; you may feel tension between proclamation and entertainment, between content and application, between appealing to the mind and the heart.

If you encounter tension, ask yourself the following question and deal with the tension according to your answer: "Is this tension due to my commitment to denominational traditions that have become personal sacred cows, or is this tension due to a fundamental disagreement with my understanding of the Holy Scriptures?" If the tension is due to denominational traditions, disregard the tension because denominational tradition is ineffective today. If the tension is due to your biblical orientation, disregard the ideas or suggestions that are causing the tension. In either case, be sure you honestly answer the question.

You do not have to be on one side or the other of this tension. You may find yourself on both sides. For example, you may find yourself asking the question, "Where do Baby Boomers cross over the line from self-fulfillment to self-centeredness?" Pursuing the answer may point out some inconsistencies in your own ministry and force you to deal with your personal sacred cows. Several aspects of your ministry may change and others may be enlarged.

An Essential Attitude Adjustment

In order to prepare to respond to this changing, diverse world of choices, mainstream Protestant congregations must make one fundamental change in attitude: we must look outward to the needs of others rather than centering our thoughts on ourselves. We must stop worrying about survival or taking care of ourselves and begin to focus on ways to care for the world. We must develop ministries that meet the needs of people who are not yet part of our congregation. We must do most of our planning, not with our members' needs in mind, but with the needs of the unchurched firmly before us. Our members must become convinced that those who lose their lives are the only ones who find them.

This change in attitude will produce vital congregations that focus on winning the unchurched to Jesus Christ; design ministries that search out and rescue the unchurched rather than maintain the institution; define faithfulness in terms of bringing people to Christ rather than by counting members or the amount of money raised; discover that it is only as God's people are involved in outreach ministries to the world that they discover the power and fulfillment offered by the Christ of faith; understand that evangelism is not a dirty word; rediscover the urgency of evangelism and mission, without abandoning commitment to human and social needs; and have compassion on villages, towns, and cities because they are like sheep without a shepherd.

The parable of the lost sheep is the parable for our times. A rediscovery of this parable revolutionizes congregations. Think what would happen in our churches if we truly did go out in search of those sheep. Think how exciting our worship services would be if we did rejoice more when people joined our churches than when we balance our budgets. What would happen in your congregation if this parable were reinterpreted as the Parable of the Incomplete Flock and your congregation acknowledged that the flock is not yet complete? Would the way your church does business change? Would you choose different people to lead your church? Would you allocate your financial resources differently? Would your actual hands-on ministries change?

INTRODUCTION

Is the Good News that Jesus Christ has come to offer us the abundant life worth making whatever changes are needed in order for that message to be heard once again and responded to by Baby Boomers in the twenty-first century? If your answer is "yes," read on. The results you enjoy from changing your attitude will more than compensate for the tension you will feel in the process.

A Road Map

This book examines seven aspects of this changing, diverse world of choices. Chapter one lays the groundwork for effectively coping with this diverse world of choice. Chapter two discusses the necessary leadership skills. Chapter three examines organizational principles that allow the church to conduct ministry. Chapter four provides basic principles and examples of rewarding ministries. Chapter five points out ways to tell Joe/Josephine why they might want to attend church. Chapter six discusses the role of developing stewardship of money. Chapter seven examines the changing aspects of worship and preaching. The Appendix contains examples of helpful material used in various churches.

I
BUILDING BRIDGES TO THE BABY BOOMERS

And it shall come to pass afterward, that I will pour out my spirit on all flesh; your sons and your daughters shall prophesy, your old men shall dream dreams, and your young men shall see visions.

Joel 2:28

We have met the enemy and he is us.

Pogo

She stood at the podium of a large denominational gathering. A distinguished woman with graying hair and careworn features, she addressed the audience: "I want you to know I am not a young adult; but I am trying to understand them."

The Baby Boomer sitting next to me commented, "I can't believe she said that." He was responding to the feelings of every other person in the audience whose birth date occurred between 1946 and 1964. The woman's tone and inflection were very condescending.

The gap between the mind-set of mainstream Protestants and Baby Boomers visiting our churches is often like the Grand Canyon. Some church members are struggling to bridge this gap. Some do not even know the gap exists. Others do their best to widen the gap.

This gap is revealed by watching the interaction between Joe/Josephine and Max/Maxine. Joe/Josephine represent the Baby Boomer, either churched or unchurched; Max/Maxine represent the members in many mainstream Protestant churches. They have different value systems and are not motivated the same way.

To determine whether you are Joe/Josephine or Max/Maxine, answer this question: "Do you pick up pennies?" Max/Maxine pick up pennies; Joe/Josephine do not. Max/Maxine think Joe/Josephine do not value money because they do not pick up pennies. Max/Maxine say pennies have value if you pick up enough of them. Joe/Josephine respond that by the time they pick up enough pennies to have any value they would have a back problem. Both value money; they just have different perspectives on what constitutes value.

The church recipe cookbook fund-raiser is a classic example of the difference in these two value systems. Many churches led by Max/Maxine still try to raise money through the sale of cookbooks. When Joe/Josephine do not participate by submitting recipes or purchasing the cookbooks, Max/Maxine get upset and wonder why they are not more committed to the church. The truth is, Joe/Josephine do not have any recipes to submit, since they seldom cook. When they do, it is in the microwave. They want instant products that almost cook themselves. Max/Maxine make the same mistake when they expect Joe/Josephine to bake cakes or cookies for the bake sale. Few Baby Boomers ever bake for themselves.

26

Women's groups composed of Maxines still insist on holding their studies in the morning. Their subject is still some distant mission study. It never dawns on them that Josephine works outside the home now. If women's groups want to reach Josephine, they need to teach potty training in the evening.

We observe the interaction between Joe/Josephine and Max/Maxine in order to encourage a narrowing of this gap in three ways: (1) help Max/Maxine develop an appreciation for Joe/Josephine; (2) introduce Super Max/Maxine and their most often used ploys against Baby Boomers and (3) describe the "Bridge Builders."

Appreciating Baby Boomers

Max/Maxine, the average church members, need to develop an appreciation for Baby Boomers (referred to from here on as Joe/Josephine). The average Max/Maxine does not have much appreciation for Joe/Josephine. Some Max/Maxines think of Joe/Josephine as strange beings from another planet who have no appreciation for the things that made America great. Some Max/Maxines even fear their existence in the church; others dismiss them as spoiled brats.

Seldom are Joe/Josephine welcomed into the power structure of the church. They are allowed to teach Sunday school or to work in the various programs of the church, but they are seldom found on the power committees such as finance, trustees, nominating, or sessions. Only under extremely rare circumstances do we see a congregation that has been in existence more than thirty years where Joe/Josephine occupy power positions such as chairperson of a major board.

Perhaps the most demoralizing effect of this lack of appreciation for Joe/Josephine occurs when they offer suggestions for new programs. No matter how well their program idea is thought through, it is often dismissed as silly or unnecessary. One of the the only ways Joe/Josephine can

27

get a new program started is by having one of the more influential Max/Maxines on their committee.

This unconscious attitude of superiority toward the younger generation is true to some extent of every generation of Americans. I can remember my father telling me how he walked barefoot to school, uphill both ways, through the snow—his way of telling me he thought I had it too easy and took too much for granted. His father probably felt the same about him. Joe/Josephine are no more different from their parents than we were from ours. If we do not keep this natural phenomenon of "generational superiority" in mind when dealing with Joe/Josephine, we may lose our perspective. How easily we mistake our own experiences and insights from the past as "eternal truths" that apply to new generations in the same way they did to ours.

We could list many reasons why Max/Maxine should appreciate Joe/Josephine. They have a passion for discovering more of life. For them life is a continuous search for significance and self-fulfillment; a process that is colored with exploration and wonder. Life is intrinsically good and therefore to be savored and enjoyed as much as possible. Life is sacred; and quality of life is a major concern. Care of the environment is of paramount importance.

In traveling through airports, I notice that the vast majority of the travelers are adults under the age of forty. A part of me wishes that I had felt free at that age to explore and experience so much of life. I felt a duty to produce at an early age. Joe/Josephine embrace the freedom to live life to the fullest. They do not have the same urgent sense of duty or obligation to be successful in a career. While personal success is a high priority, Joe/Josephine focus on the process of discovering more about life itself.

Joe/Josephine are passionate about this search. They demonstrate genuine excitement when they discover new sensations. They do not have their parents' compulsion to be inhibited. Their passion for life makes Joe/Josephine exciting people who are open to new ideas and fun to be around. Their search inevitably drives them toward people. The individualism of the 1970s is beginning to soften, as maturity produces a growing need for community. Relationships are more important than rules. Family, marriage, and home are essential elements of their search. Male and female are seen as equals. Education becomes a way of life. Global concerns are as important as local issues.

Joe/Josephine have much to offer mainstream Protestantism. Max/Maxine need not fear or ignore them. Church leaders find it in their best interest to fully embrace Joe/Josephine and welcome them into the congregation. Without them, mainstream churches are not just less effective; they will increasingly become marginal members of a society that views them as obsolete.

However, not all is well with Joe/Josephine. In spite of all the reasons for appreciating them, they have one major flaw that cannot be overlooked. No matter how positively we describe them, it is impossible to overstate their preoccupation with self. Whether we call this trait self-fulfillment or self-centeredness, we cannot alter the fact that Joe/Josephine are extremely focused on themselves and proud of it.

In reaching out to Joe/Josephine, mainstream churches cannot avoid dealing with this self-centeredness. The secret of a good ministry to Joe/Josephine cannot be measured by how many of them join our churches, but by how many move from a preoccupation with self to a commitment to the mission of Jesus Christ.

Super Max/Maxine

Super Max/Maxine are one of the primary obstacles in the way of Joe/Josephine joining mainstream churches. Super Max/Maxine say they want the church to grow, but they really do not mean it. Super Max/Maxine are big fish in a little pond, and they want to remain that way. They hold only those offices in the church that have power; and they welcome Joe/Josephine into the church only if they enter on Super Max/Maxine's terms and perpetuate their values. The church belongs to Super Max/Maxine, not to

God. Christ is not the center of their lives; they are. Their needs and values are more important than those of Christ or the church.

Most churches have a small group of well-entrenched Super Max/Maxines. The good news is that each church contains only a few of them. The bad news is that they are usually allowed to dominate and control the decision-making processes. Super Max/Maxine fill the major decision-making committees in our churches, while they allow Joe and Josephine to fill the working committees of the church such as teaching Sunday school, sponsoring the youth groups, or singing in the choir. Super Max/Maxine are allowed to keep a tight grip on the church even when the majority of the members know they are wrong! This happens because most church members would rather be nice and avoid controversy than to demonstrate Christian concern and ask Super Max/Maxine to step aside or share power.

Super Max/Maxine are portrayed in the Bible by the elder brother in the parable of the prodigal son. Instead of rejoicing with the father when his younger brother came to his senses and returned home, the elder brother complained. He knew that accepting back his younger brother meant that his position at home would have to change. He knew that he would have to share his father's love with someone else. And the elder brother was too self-centered to allow that to happen. So the elder brother raised the roof, just like Super Max/Maxine raise the roof when Joe/Josephine attempt to return home.

A young pastor recently wrote me a lengthy letter detailing his frustrations with the ministry. "Up until recently, I thought that virtually any church with a strong leader, a fair location, and human beings living nearby had growth potential." Now he was not so sure. He went on to say that one of the reasons why the church he just moved from was dying was the mind-set and attitude of a small handful of members. They had fought every effort he made to help the church grow. As I read the letter, I felt the pain and anguish of this young pastor. The members he described were the Super Max/Maxines.

If mainstream Protestant churches are to reach Baby Boomers for Christ, Super Max/Maxine either have to be converted or held accountable for the Joe/Josephines they drive away from the church. Who is responsible for dealing with Max/Maxine? Everyone! Super Max/Maxine thrive on the silence of the majority. They take that silence as tacit support for their views. The more members are involved in either converting or holding Max/Maxine accountable, the less likely they are to divide and conquer the membership and derail significant change. Should it prove to be impossible to convert or hold Max/Maxine accountable, then they should be avoided and excluded from leadership roles.

Do not equate such accountability with a lack of love for Super Max/Maxine. The other members are not showing love for Super Max/Maxine by allowing their actions to stifle church vitality. Biblical love is shown by holding Max/Maxine accountable for their actions and helping them see a Christian way to live their lives. Christian love is not shown by being silent; Christian love is shown by exposing their actions and requiring them to get honest or get out!

How does a pastor or lay person begin to cope with Super Max/Maxine? Three suggestions prove helpful. First, discover a small group of committed, core leaders who understand the problem of Super Max/Maxine and want to do something about it. This group does not have to be more than three or four long-time respected members who do more than their share of the work and financial support. Next, nurture these leaders into a cohesive group whose sole purpose is to convert or remove Super Max/Maxine from power. The group must understand that love must permeate all they do, and conflict is inevitable. Finally, put this group in as many power positions as possible and equip them to take the lead in the struggle.

In order to discover who Super Max/Maxine really are, let us examine some of Super Max/Maxine's favorite statements. Do not be alarmed if some of these ploys sound familiar. No one is perfect. Decide how you feel about the statement and enter the appropriate number. Rate yourself on a scale of one to ten. One means that you totally agree with the statement. Ten means that you totally disagree with the statement and have no desire to change your attitude.

"Not in my pew you don't." We all laugh about the church members who sit in the same pew every Sunday and when unsuspecting visitors sit in their seat, they ask them to move. That attitude is no joke. Turf issues of all kinds are tearing many churches apart: Sunday school classes that are unwilling to move from "their" room so that the church can better utilize space; parking spaces that belong to certain members; and members who insist on holding the same office in the church for years.

One church spent a considerable amount of money on a church parlor. It was an immaculate room, but it was also a source of serious alienation between Max/Maxine and Joe/Josephine. Children were not welcome in the parlor because they made it dirty. In addition, the parlor was not used on Sunday, even though the church needed Sunday school space for children. Turf issues are a theological, not an architectural matter. They are outward expressions of our inward sin: self-centeredness.

How do you feel about the italicized statement below?

Turf issues are harmful to the growth of a church.

1	2	3	4	5	6	7	8	9	10

"It was good enough for my children." Super Max/Maxine never understand the need for a nicer and better nursery, staffed by paid people, and open every time the church has a function. The nursery was good enough for them, and it should be good enough for Joe/Josephine. More often than not, parlors and offices are nicer than the nursery. The nursery often doubles as a storeroom. In many places parents have to plead for the nursery to be open at times other than Sunday morning.

Super Max/Maxine fail to realize that families have fewer children today and value quality child care. Super

Max/Maxine's mother would leave her third or fourth child in any flat comfortable spot. But today's mother in her late twenties or early thirties with only one child is very particular about where she leaves that child.

How do you feel about the following statement?

The nursery should be extra clean, neat, staffed with paid help, and open every time there is a church function.

1	2	3	4	5	6	7	8	9	10

"Let's keep the facilities clean." This sounds reasonable, until you begin to develop ministries for children or allow the community to use the facilities on a regular basis. Super Max/Maxine take more pride in the beauty of the facilities than in the people who might be ministered to in those facilities. One of the most often used excuses for not opening up the church facilities to the community is that the people who use them do not take care of them. That is probably true. But who cares, if using the facilities results in a stronger ministry to the community and a stronger church? Are facilities more important than people? They are very important to Super Max/Maxine.

A young church built a gymnasium. At first, they tried to keep a tight rein on who used the facility. It did stay looking nice, but there was a lot of vandalism. They decided to open the gym from morning until late night and let the community use it simply by signing up. The vandalism stopped. The facilities began to look used, but over the years the activities in that gym have more than paid for the facility in the goodwill, visibility, and the new members who have joined that church through the athletic ministries.

Not long ago I drove by a church that had several small signs on the lawn: "Stay off the Grass!" "Don't Cut Across Here!" "No Trespassing!" Not far from the church I serve, in a neighborhood that is exceptionally free from vandalism, a church erected a chain link fence all around its property. On the fence, facing the street, these words are printed in big letters: Stanley Smith Security. Twenty years ago, this church was larger than the church I serve. Today, it is a tiny, struggling congregation. What they saved in vandalism and burglaries they have lost many times over in new members who might have joined were it not for the fence that remains locked part of the day.

How do you feel about the following statement?

I'm willing for the facilities to be used even if they get dirty.

1	2	3	4	5	6	7	8	9	10

"Before we go out after new members, let's take better care of our own members. We have so many inactives. We ought to see how many of them we can bring back into the church before we try to get any more new members." Do not be deceived by this ploy. Super Max/Maxine have no intention of taking better care of the members. If they did, they would have done that long ago. Most churches take very poor care of their members; otherwise, more of them would still be involved in the life of the church. Super Max/Maxine know many of the inactives and know that they are not a threat to their authority if they return. The hidden motive (often hidden even to Super Max/Maxine) is to control who joins the church. They do not want a lot of strangers interfering in their well-organized church. (They also know from earlier experiences that very few of the inactives will ever return.)

Super Max/Maxine refuse to acknowledge that the best way to nurture the present membership is to get the membership to reach out to others. Christian nurture is never seen as taking better care of the church. Christian nurture and evangelism are one and the same, because as we nurture others we nurture ourselves.

How do you feel about the following statement?

Reaching out to new members is just as important as taking care of the present members.

1	2	3	4	5	6	7	8	9	10

"But we've always done it this way." Not long ago, the pastors of a church in Texas decided to stop wearing robes in worship. Not long after that decision was made, they received this letter:

> I have noticed you no longer wear robes in church. I'm not sure of all your reasons, but I object. Your attempts to "grow" at the expense of maintaining traditions is wrong. If you cannot return to tradition and maintain growth too, I intend to leave your church.

This person cares more about keeping the status quo than discovering new ways of reaching Joe/Josephine. Super Max/Maxine do not want change for two reasons: (1) They do not know what the changes will do to their ability to control the church; and (2) They have a great investment in their own spiritual comfort, which is fed more by familiarity than by discovery of new ideas.

In 1990, a church in Oklahoma changed some of its terminology—simple things like calling the sanctuary the celebration center, the narthex the foyer, the education building the Christian life center, and the bulletin the program. Some members left the church over these simple, nonessential changes. They had more invested in tradition than in mission.

In a very short time tradition can replace mission. The legalistic tradition of the Pharisees that Jesus challenged was less than ninety-five years old. We find no records of the Pharisees 100 years before Christ.

How do you feel about the following statement?

I am comfortable with radical change if it will help my church reach more people for Christ.

1	2	3	4	5	6	7	8	9	10

"But the rules say . . ." Super Max/Maxine are more concerned about parliamentary procedure and rules than ministry to people. Meetings break down and decisions are delayed because something is not done just right. Super

Max/Maxine know how to disrupt the flow of a meeting by manipulation of the rules. Super Max/Maxine delay crucial decisions by saying the motion has not gone through the proper committees or channels.

How do you feel about the following statement?

I am seldom concerned about procedure.

1	2	3	4	5	6	7	8	9	10

"Let's pay the debt off first." Many churches mortgage their future because Super Max/Maxine are more concerned about paying off small debts than about starting needed ministries or providing more space or curriculum for Sunday school. To them, the memories of the Great Depression are more impressive than the grace of God. Their emphasis is on worrying about paying off "small debts," rather than finding ways to reach more people (small debt is anything less then 10 percent of a church's budget).

How do you feel about the following statement?

Paying off the debt is not a major concern to me.

1	2	3	4	5	6	7	8	9	10

"Don't touch those CDs." Most dying churches have money in the bank. Money in the bank for a "rainy day" is more important to Super Max/Maxine than starting new ministries that serve members and reach new people. If someone suggests spending some of this money in order to arrest the decline and provide a foundation for the future, Super Max/Maxine go berserk. The money must be guarded at all costs. In many cases, enough money is in the bank to take care of the facilities long after all the people are dead and buried or have moved to a church that is still alive. Thus, the money is a spiritual neutron bomb that provides a false sense of security to those who place more importance on security than on winning people to Jesus Christ.

How do you feel about the following statement?

Let's spend some of the CDs to hire more staff or start new programs.

1	2	3	4	5	6	7	8	9	10

"But I want to know everyone." One of the most often heard excuses for not starting a second or third service on Sunday morning, or a second adult Sunday school class is that the members will no longer know everyone. Super Max/Maxine often view the church as a family reunion. They go to church to catch up on the community gossip. Their primary concern on Sunday is to renew acquaintances, rather than to worship God. They are more concerned about the sentimental feelings they experience at the church than they are about whether or not the church is actively sharing the Good News. Sure, we go to church for the community we find there, but if that is the primary reason, we have missed the whole point of worship.

How do you feel about the following statement?

Several worship services are fine with me because I am more interested in meeting the needs of all the people than I am in knowing everyone at church.

1	2	3	4	5	6	7	8	9	10

"The pastor hasn't been to my home in months." Super Max/Maxine view their pastor as their personal chaplain. They get very upset when the pastor does not visit them regularly, even if nothing is wrong. When the pastor fails to visit regularly, Super Max/Maxine make things so uncomfortable for everyone that the pastor either gives in or faces serious consequences. Some pastors spend so much time taking care of a handful of church members that there is not much time left to take care of the quiet majority, much less to be any kind of a witness in the world.

The Bible does not paint this kind of picture of pastoral ministry. It says that the role of the pastor is to equip, train, and lead the laity into ministry, both within and outside the church. It is not the role of the pastor to be anyone's personal chaplain.

How do you feel about the following statement?

I'm not at all offended when my pastor does not give me regular personal attention.

1	2	3	4	5	6	7	8	9	10

"Why do we need so many staff?" Super Max/Maxine still think that all programs can and should be run by volunteers. Staff is seen as a threat to their power. Super Max/Maxine have no idea how complex life is today. They have not considered that in most households both spouses work outside the home. In our present complex quality-oriented world where time is as valuable as money, most ongoing ministries must be supervised by paid staff. Super Max/Maxine think that staff takes the place of volunteers. They do not understand that more staff means more volunteers. They are not aware of the studies indicating that each additional staff member can mean up to 150 new members.

How do you feel about the following statement?

I realize that more staff is needed today than in the past.

1	2	3	4	5	6	7	8	9	10

"It's just another gimmick to help pay for the budget." Super Max/Maxine have a hard time understanding that the primary mission of the church is to equip them to win others to Jesus Christ. They are fixated on the belief that the church centers around their needs. So when the pastor pushes evangelism, Super Max/Maxine feel they are being manipulated. They cling to the idea that the primary mission of the church is to nurture them and those like them.

How do you feel about the following statement?

I always trust and affirm my pastor's efforts to reach more people for Christ.

1	2	3	4	5	6	7	8	9	10

Total up your score and divide by twelve. If your average score is higher than four, you are on your way to becoming a Super Max/Maxine. The more your average score goes over four, the more closely you resemble Super Max/Maxine. If your average score is over seven, you are a hard-core Super Max/Maxine.

Bridge Builders

One of the desperate needs of most mainstream congregations is a group of people whose primary responsibility is that of building bridges between Max/Maxine and Joe/Josephine—people who work to break Super Max/Maxine's control of the church and to incorporate Joe/Josephine into the power structure of the church. Their mission is not easy. Although studies show that the best bridge builders are people born in the 1930s, their age is not as important as whether these people are: (1) open, tolerant, and loving; (2) in love with Jesus Christ and his mission of salvation more than they love themselves or their church; (3) willing to put the spiritual needs of others before their own; and (4) willing to rely more on the power of the Holy Spirit than on themselves in order to accomplish their almost impossible bridge-building task.

The goal of bridge building is three-fold: First, bridge builders want to provide a tolerant, hospitable environment, which clearly acknowledges that all of God's children (no matter what age) are of equal value, are respected, and are welcome at this church. Bridge builders know that both young and old have mixed feelings about their aging process. Joe/Josephine have extremely negative feelings about growing older, and they allow these feelings to get in the way of communicating with Max/Maxine. On the other hand, Max/Maxine do not handle well the fact that they are becoming more vulnerable, both to the aging process and to the changing roles they must anticipate. To them, retirement suggests becoming non-productive; seniority implies less visibility; and those who once paid the bills now fear the loss of autonomy and self-control. Such changes cause a breakdown in communication because of latent anger.

Second, bridge builders try to discover the common denominator between Joe/Josephine and Max/Maxine. Bridge builders try to concentrate on what the two generations have in common rather than their differences. These common interests, even though they are expressed somewhat differently, are love, home, family, and a meaningful life.

Third, bridge builders try to provide opportunities for both generations to work together. Depending on how many hard-core Max/Maxines a church has, these opportunities range from the basic exchange of pleasantries, to sharing tasks and problem solving, to the exchange of actual feelings, to opportunities where dreams, hopes, needs, and fears are the focus of the communication. What then are the tools by which the bridge builders achieve their goals?

The primary tool for reaching Max/Maxine is to appeal to their sense of duty and obligation. Max/Maxine are materialistic beings. They have a strong work ethic and take pride in doing their best. All they need is a valid reason to open their arms to Joe/Josephine. Help them understand that turning over power to Joe/Josephine determines whether or not all their hard work continues after they are dead. Max/Maxine have invested years and money in their church and do not want to see the church die. Most of them are experiencing pain over the decline of their church.

Another helpful way to use this tool is to show Max/Maxine that decisions to increase the mission of the church are good financial investments. The smaller the church becomes, the more money and time Max/Maxine have to give for the upkeep of the facilities, and the less money there is for missions. Max/Maxine respond to bottom-line goals.

Another angle is to remind Max/Maxine that their own children are more prone to participate in the life of a church when the older members are open to their way of doing things. Many Max/Maxines have deep-seated guilt because their children no longer attend church. They wonder what they did wrong as parents. They long for the day when their children return to the church. Help them to see how they can play a constructive part in achieving that goal.

If more altruistic ways exist to reach Max/Maxine, I have not found them. Max/Maxine's faith is individualistic, private, and formed around their own needs. The Word of God is not the primary source of decision making in their lives. Instead, personal opinion and social pressures influence most of their decisions. In their own way, Max/Maxine are just as preoccupied with self as are Joe/Josephine. How easily we forget that we are all sinners.

The primary tool for reaching Joe/Josephine is an appeal to their compassion and their need for meaning in life. Joe/Josephine need to discover that by giving themselves to others they will find the self-fulfillment and abundant life that they seek. They need to discover that: (1) joy comes to those who live life on behalf of others; (2) self-denial does not mean the denial of life; (3) celebration is a regular part of church worship and ministry; and (4) compassion for others rather than commitment to the church is the goal of discipleship. In order to accomplish these objectives, the church needs to provide a variety of short-term ministry opportunities that help Joe/Josephine find more meaning in their lives. The only way Max/Maxine can discover what kind of new ministries their church needs to start is by listening to the suggestions given by Joe/Josephine.

What can Max/Maxine and Joe/Josephine learn from each other? Joe/Josephine can teach Max/Maxine that: (1) they do not have to deny life in order to live by the ethic of self-denial; (2) human life and planet Earth are sacred; (3) part of being human is knowing that it is appropriate to express emotion, even in church; and (4) work and play are both an integral part of a balanced life.

Max/Maxine can teach Joe/Josephine that: (1) the pursuit of instant gratification is not compatible with growing older; (2) the importance of commitment has not changed even in a throw-away society where nothing lasts very long; (3) some things in life are worth waiting for; (4) beauty is in the eye of the beholder; and (5) death is a natural part of life.

Max/Maxine must, however, understand that they carry the primary responsibility for bridge building. If Max/Maxine do not initiate bridge building, Joe/Josephine quietly leave or continue to avoid mainstream churches. That is not just Joe/Josephine's loss, or mainstream Protestantism's loss; it is the kingdom's loss.

Max/Maxine must be willing to reach out to Joe/Josephine and provide them an extended family—to fully embrace them into the church. Accomplishing this is not easy, but it can happen.

Operative Words for Reaching Baby Boomers

The following list summarizes most of what we need to know in order to develop ministries that reach Joe/Josephine. This list forms the framework for understanding the ideas and methods advocated in the rest of the book.

BASICS—Churches need to return to the basics of faith and teach more Bible.

BELONGING—Even though Joe/Josephine are not "joiners," they have a deep desire to belong.

BUSY—Time is now as important as money.

CHILD CARE—Joe/Josephine expect the church to provide quality child care.

CHOICES—Joe/Josephine have diverse life-styles that require a wide range of options.

CONNECTEDNESS—The more we rely on computers and the more specialized the work force becomes, the more

Joe/Josephine experience the need to be connected to the whole.

CONSULTATIVE—Program planning needs to be done with Joe/Josephine, not for them.

DEATH—Over the next twenty-five years Joe/Josephine's mortality will consume more and more of their time.

ELECTRONIC—Homes today are filled with electronics.

EMOTIONAL—Joe/Josephine live more by the heart than by the head, making celebration and love of life highly important to them.

EXPERIMENTAL—In a changing world, churches need to risk a lot of trial and error.

FAMILY—The major source of ministries to reach Joe/Josephine involve the family.

FAST—Joe/Josephine live a fast-paced life and have a short interest span.

FLEXIBLE—Those who work with Joe/Josephine must see life as a process or pilgrimage rather than static and concrete.

FUTURE-ACTIVE LEADERSHIP—Church leaders who wish to attract Joe/Josephine sniff out and respond to world changes before they happen.

HEROS—They have none since the death of Robert Kennedy and Martin Luther King, Jr.

HOMEBOUND—Joe/Josephine enjoy staying home.

INCENTIVES—Joe/Josephine must be able to see how participation in a church can benefit them.

INFORMAL—Formality is out in everything.

INFORMATION—Joe/Josephine expect a full disclosure of all matters.

INNOVATIVE—The more Max/Maxine are comfortable with change, the more open the church is to Joe/Josephine.

HOW TO REACH BABY BOOMERS

LEADERSHIP—Strong leaders attract Joe/Josephine.

MAINSTREET U.S.A.—Joe/Josephine long for the warm feelings that come from the small town atmosphere and a emphasis on community.

MISSIONS—The more money a church invests in missions and the more hands-on opportunities for mission, the more likely it is that Joe/Josephine are involved in the church.

NETWORKS—Joe/Josephine like to feel part of a larger community.

OPPRESSION—Joe/Josephine appreciate a pastor who speaks out against all forms of oppression.

OUTSIDE IN—Ideas for new ministries need to come from outside the church rather than from within.

PERSONALIZED—Generic programs from the top down will not speak to the needs of today.

POLITICS—They have little interest in this, and yet 1992 will be the first year their voice is heard in a major way.

PRACTICAL—"How to" is more important than theory.

RECREATIONAL—Athletics are an everyday part of Joe/Josephine's world.

RELATIONSHIPS—Establishing lasting relationships is a major drive for Joe/Josephine.

SELF-FULFILLMENT—Searching for significance occupies much of Joe/Josephine's time.

SERVICE—Opportunities need to be provided for personal involvement in service to others.

SHORT-TERM—Joe/Josephine are reluctant to make long-term commitments.

SIMPLICITY—Look for ways to simplify this complex world.

SINGLE— Many spend a large portion of their life single.

SOCIAL/FELLOWSHIP—Joe/Josephine thrive on fellowship.

SPIRITUAL FORMATION—Prayer and support groups are helpful.

STABILITY—Pastors need to stay at one church longer.

STRATEGIC—Churches must decide who their target audience is.

STRESS—They are the first generation that cannot expect a higher standard of living than their parents. Two incomes per family are viewed as essential.

SUNSET—Many traditional ministries of the church need to be discontinued.

TEAM EFFORT—Joe/Josephine like to work in teams rather than as individuals.

TOLERANT—Not even the AIDS epidemic can dampen Joe/Josephine's tolerance toward others.

TRAVEL—Joe/Josephine travel more than other generations, and much of it is on the weekend.

UNPREDICTABLE—So much change is occurring today that all predictions are unpredictable (except this one).

VALUE/QUALITY—Appearance is important and mediocrity is avoided.

VIETNAM—The disillusionment of this war is considered by many Joe/Josephines as the most memorable event in their lives.

This book examines the implication of these words for the church.

II
FUTURE-ACTIVE LEADERSHIP

The greater the emphasis on broad-based partici-pation (participatory democracy) in planning and decision making, the more difficult it is to initiate and implement changes from within the organiza-tion.

Lyle Schaller

A new style of leadership is required to build bridges in a changing, diverse world of choices. This new leadership can be described as "future-active." Five words define future-active leadership: open, fast, flexible, deci-sive, and innovative. This leadership initiates rather than manages or coordinates. It takes risks, rather than main-tains the status quo. It encourages people to attempt things they might not do on their own. The day of the "enabler" leadership model is over. The only thing the enabler enables today is the death of congregations.

Seven obstacles stand in the way when future-active leadership is attempted in the parish: (1) familiarity with the status quo; (2) the present leadership's lack of openness to change; (3) older leadership's unwillingness to learn new skills; (4) leadership's insistence on maintaining the institution more than ministering to people; (5) lack of belief in the importance of the church; (6) availability of money to keep the institutional systems running; and (7) an unwillingness to allow Joe/Josephine into major power positions. This chapter examines how future-active leadership overcomes these seven obstacles.

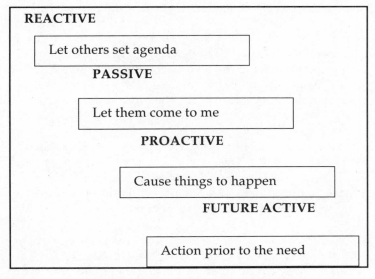

Figure 1

Future-active leaders anticipate and embrace change. Figure 1 depicts four types of leadership. The first type is "reactive leadership." These leaders react to the actions of someone or something else, and they allow others to set the agenda for the church. The attempts by mainstream denominations to stop their membership declines reflect a reactive leadership style.

"Passive leadership" sits back and waits for the unchurched to come to the church or for problems to go away. Passive leadership avoids the use of power or authority and takes action only when forced. In the void caused by such leadership, Super Max/Maxine often control the congregation. Much of mainstream leadership falls into the reactive or passive categories.

A third type of leadership is "proactive." These leaders cause things to happen that do not otherwise happen. Until recently, this type of leadership was effective. However, this changing, diverse world of choices is moving so fast and mainstream churches are so far behind in addressing change that proactive leadership is no longer effective.

"Future-active" leadership is needed today. Michael Kami describes this new leadership as "Detectives of Change," "Architects of Change," and "Agents of Change." [1] Future-active leaders thrive on becoming familiar with the unfamiliar. They enjoy change and embrace chaos. They are comfortable with situations they do not understand. Uncharted water is no more of a challenge to them than a study of past history.

Future-active leaders are alert to the rapidly shifting changes in culture. They analyze the way things are and interpret what they mean to the church in the future. Demographic trends and sociological changes stimulate them to plan strategies that lay foundations for future ministries.

Future-active leaders think as creatively in their leadership at church as they do in the world of business. They are secure enough to be open to change; sensible enough to apply common sense in their designs for ministry; innovative enough to plan ministries that meet the day-to-day needs of both the membership and the unchurched; and have enough relationships throughout the church to cause changes to become reality within the structure of the church.

Future-active leaders are open to and comfortable with diversity. Today's leaders are confronted with a diversity not present three decades ago. They contend with the wide gulf between Max/Maxine and Joe/Josephine; those reared in the church and those not reared in the church; those who grew up in their denomination and those who grew up in other denominations. The variety of life-styles among contemporary Americans further enhances this diversity. The manner in which pastors and laity relate to this dramatically increased diversity determines much of the health of the church. And more powerful than any other determiner, whether a leader views diversity as a curse or an opportunity depends on his or her ministry goals. If, for example, the leader's goal is maintaining the institution or making denominational converts out of visitors and members, diversity gets in the way. Although essential to reaching Joe/Josephine, an attitude of openness and the affirmation of diversity erode denominational loyalty. Denominations were established to conserve tradition, not to change it. Pastors who try to mold people into good members of the denomination will find diversity either a threat or a time-consuming chore. Their struggle with this will block their ability to thrive on the multitude of opportunities for new ministries fostered by diversity and pluralism. If, however, a leader's goal is developing loyalty to Christ rather than loyalty to the denomination, diversity becomes a wondrous joy that makes that goal easier to reach.

Future-active leaders approach diversity as something to be embraced, encouraged, and celebrated rather than something to be overcome or molded into a system. Tolerance of diversity is not enough! These new leaders openly bless a wide range of gifts, graces, and life-styles. They encourage each unique individual to find her or his place within God's world. Congregational unity is found in a common commitment to Jesus Christ rather than in requiring everyone to think alike. Future-active leaders stop beating the institutional drums and start fostering personal relationships with Jesus Christ. This does not mean that the new leaders discard the denomination, rather that it loses its role as the guiding light of ministry.

Embracing diversity does not mean that a church is without standards for measuring faithfulness. But these stan-

dards are not racial, gender, denominational, or national—
or whether one is liberal, fundamental, or moderate. For
example, the changing role of women and the homosexual-
ity debate are only two of many significant issues emerging
in our pluralistic society. Some church leaders allow singu-
lar issues such as these to fill their agendas. Standards of
the Christian faith, however, cannot be tied to any one culture, form of government, or denominational value system.
When that happens, as it has in the United States and
Europe in this century, the impact of Christianity is lost as
soon as you step outside the influence of that particular
thought form.

Future-active leaders embrace diversity by using four
universal and ancient guidelines to measure the faithfulness of God's people: the cross, confession, forgiveness,
and the community of faith. People experience the cross,
express confession, receive and give forgiveness, and live
in community in many different ways. But none of these
can be held captive in boxes labeled gender, race, creed,
nationality, or theological orientation.

Today's diversity is an expression of divine creation. God
created each of us differently. As we celebrate this diversity, the problems of race, gender, creed, nationalism, and
theological orientation are supplanted by the wonder of
God's creative activity.

In addition to the four theological measuring sticks—the
cross, confession, forgiveness, and the community of
faith—future-active leaders provide the psychological and
sociological glue that holds together the extreme diversity
of contemporary congregations. Mainstream churches need
cohesive leadership that has a vision of what can be rather
than what is or has been; a balanced personal ministry that
covers the spectrum of religious experience and expression;
flexibility in matters that are not essential to faith; clarity
about one's own standards and a willingness to objectively
share them without appearing to be the sole possessor of
truth; an openness to new ideas; a healthy curiosity about
how life works; trust in the competency and integrity of coworkers; strong organizational skills; a secure sense of self-

worth; and the courage to use that influence for the common good of the church. By the power of God's grace, future-active leaders accomplish this impossible but essential ministry of cohesive leadership in congregations more diverse than any since Corinth.

Future-active leaders give clear directions and then get out of the way. Most young adults are predicted to be community volunteers by 1995 (many already are). Joe/Josephine expect to volunteer for a clearly defined mission that is important to the overall health of the church. Once this direction is given, future-active leaders step back and allow Joe/Josephine to take full responsibility for the outcome. When leaders do not use this approach, Joe/Josephine take their volunteering elsewhere.

Mission statements are an excellent way of providing these directions. Mission statements define the church's elusive "bottom line" as people; encourage innovative ideas; help people understand why the objectives need to be implemented; ensure that the various ministries of the church support and enhance the goals of the church; and let people know when to celebrate the completion of the task. Mission statements are needed for: (1) the church as a whole, (2) each lay ministry, and (3) each paid staff.

A mission statement for the church as a whole provides a context in which all of the actions of the church are evaluated. This statement needs to be clear, concise, open-ended, and short enough to be remembered and used as part of worship. One example of a mission statement for a church: "We are the people of God, called to live under the umbrella of love, justice, and mercy, to nurture the churched and to win the unchurched."

Each lay ministry needs a mission statement that spells out its objectives and the level of support to be expected from the church. An example of the mission statement used at Colonial Hills United Methodist Church for teaching in the Sunday school is found in Appendix One. The statement explains that teaching is the means to an end, rather than the goal, and spells out *what* must happen in the classroom, rather than *how* it must happen.

51

Mission statements are required for paid staff. Today's complex environment, coupled with denominations more interested in maintenance than ministry, make mission statements essential to productive ministry. However, most churches do not provide them. When they do, they are usually too vague to be of any benefit. When specific and measurable, they are usually for office personnel rather than for program staff. This tells us one of three things about the leadership: either clerical work is valued more than ministry; or leaders do not understand that mission statements are essential in a complex, specialized society; or we are too lazy or unfocused to provide the more difficult mission statements for program staff.

All three observations appear applicable. Two things happen in a maintenance-oriented organization: (1) paper work takes precedence over people; and (2) anyone is viewed as capable of doing the work. If maintaining the institution is the goal, it does not matter who does what or how well they do it. All that matters is that there are enough people to be around when needed. Nothing else needs to be done to preside over the maintenance of a dying institution.

A sample mission statement for the minister of music is provided in the appendix. An examination of this document reveals the following basic elements: The mission statement is written prior to hiring; it distinguishes between the important items on which the person is evaluated and the everyday routine responsibilities; it is written from the perspective of the overall goals of the church; the music ministry is viewed as an expanding venture rather than maintenance of an existing ministry; 10 percent of the priority matters are left to be filled in by the new staff person; the minister of music is accountable only to the senior pastor; how the objectives are to be accomplished is left up to the staff person; and the document is written by the senior pastor. Some of these observations require explanation.

Staff mission statements are written before hiring staff or selecting lay people to ensure that the objectives support the overall goals of the church. Missions statements are not intended to control or to make staff into "gofers." They are intended to help staff function on behalf of the spiritual health of the entire church, rather than on behalf of their particular portion of it.

Paid staff should be allowed to fill out 10 percent of the mission statements for their positions. This action shows confidence in the person; gives the person the opportunity to have ownership in the mission statement; and gives the supervisor an idea of what interests this person.

Staff mission statements also spell out productive lines of authority. If the paid staff consists of more than two full-time clergy or program people, the personnel committee evaluates only the senior pastor. It is far more difficult for a senior pastor to motivate or hold staff accountable when a committee evaluates the staff. Each staff member is evaluated by and accountable to the senior pastor or other designated staff person and has access to the personnel committee only by request. Volunteer personnel committees made up of church members do not have enough daily contact with the staff to be their supervisors or to hold them accountable.

Future-active leaders motivate unpaid staff to do more than they think they are capable of accomplishing. Joe/Josephine have the highest expectations of any generation in America's history. Yet they are falling short of their dream and they know it. Joe/Josephine's search for the abundant life includes the self-fulfillment that comes from productivity and performance. They are not finding this fulfillment in the mediocrity of today's workplace. They look for it in the church, and if they find it there, they blossom. If they do not, they disappear.

Today's volunteers demand a high degree of accountability and evaluation. They want to learn from their service to others and apply it to other areas of their life. In volunteering, they are searching for meaning for themselves as much as helping others. Joe/Josephine desire opportunities to move from one challenging opportunity to an even greater challenge. Because they expect opportunities for advancement, many non-profit organizations have developed career ladders for their volunteers.

Today's volunteers are no longer well-meaning amateurs; they are well-trained and often professional unpaid staff members. When asked why they volunteer, many respond, "Because there is not enough challenge in my job." In Max/Maxine's day the philosophy of non-profit organizations was, "We do not pay volunteers so we cannot demand much." Today, successful organizations say, "Because we do not pay, we must demand even more." Today's volunteers will not stay planted where they are not growing.

Future-active leaders do not flinch from motivating the congregation to exercise its faith. Mainstream leadership has downplayed motivation and has often confused it with manipulation. But motivation is not manipulation. Motivation is the transference of emotional energy from one person to another. If people believe strongly in something, they are more apt to try to share their feelings with others. Future-active leaders believe strongly in other people's ability to do things they never dreamed possible. They take seriously Jesus' words in John 14:12: "He who believes in me will also do the works that I do; and greater works than these will he do, because I go to the Father."

Max/Maxine need motivation. They have lived in a dying congregation more than two decades. Their only context for ministry is either their nostalgic memories of what the church used to be or the condition the church is in now. Future-active leaders help them see a vision of what their church can be, and motivate them to make those visions come true.

Future-active leaders share leadership with Joe/Josephine. Young adults expect to see others their own age in leadership roles, and they respond best to leadership their own age. They expect Max/Maxine to share authority and to trust them to make changes, begin new ministries, and share in the financial decisions. Max/Maxine can remain a vital part of leadership by sharing their enormous wealth of knowledge and financial ability. But unless they are willing to give authority along with knowledge, Max/Maxine will become very lonely and weary of carrying the whole load.

Delegation of authority is the key to the successful development of leadership in a Baby Boomer world. Joe/Josephine want to know what the leadership desires to happen in the church, and they want to know what the leadership wants their role to be. But they expect the freedom to carry out their ministry in ways that meet their needs. They do not like to be closely managed.

The formula for this delegation is "resource, train, and be available." Today's volunteers do not want to plan ministry as much as they desire to carry out ministry. They expect carefully developed goals, helpful hints, and adequate materials to do a job of high quality. They need regular opportunities to explore the Scripture, acquaint themselves with church history and the basics of how their church functions. Also, they want to know that if they need help a paid staff member or pastor is always close at hand. Continuing education is expected. Often, this training can be given by the Max/Maxines—providing they can share knowledge without succumbing to the temptation to control the decision-making process.

Future-active pastors reconcile people to God rather than become co-dependent on the need to be needed. The leadership role of the pastor is in a class all its own and deserves special attention. Pastors are not professionals who help people feel better about themselves. They do not enter the ministry primarily because they have a desire to help others. Their mission is to reconcile people to God.

Many clergy confuse helping people find forgiveness and reconciliation with helping people feel better about themselves. Helping people establish a relationship with God is vastly different from helping people feel good about themselves. Some pastors have a deep-seated desire to be needed and liked which they try to satisfy through their ministries. But in the process of helping others, they become dependent on others needing their help. Their ministry becomes a form of codependency rather than an agent of divine reconciliation with God.

Codependent pastors find future-active leadership impossible. Tough decisions that affect lives or anger members are seldom made because they are not popular. Super Max/Maxine are never converted or held in check. Staff who are unwilling to grow along with the church and become nonproductive are not terminated. Pastors with an intense desire to please everyone find this changing, diverse world of choices frustrating, sometimes even defeating. Their morale is destroyed. The joy of ministry is drained from them.

On the other hand, future-active pastors, absorbed with a call to reconcile, do not get bruised egos or lose themselves in substance abuse so easily. Their morale remains high; time is too valuable and the mission to the unchurched too great to be otherwise.

The call to reconcile is greater and more profound than all the stresses of the ministry. Future-active pastors are absorbed in building bridges to God. They belong to something far greater than their own needs. When they feel low or sorry for themselves, they remember the day God said, "You shall be my witnesses in Jerusalem and in all Judea and Samaria and to the end of the earth" (Acts 1:8b). Every time they think about quitting, they remember that they are not their own, but are called by God. When floundering over the direction of their life, they remember that they have a mission of reconciliation.

Moses is an illustration of future-active pastoral leadership shaped by a mission to reconcile. Moses had a mission to free the Hebrew slaves and lead them to Canaan. Everything about his life revolved around that understanding of what God wanted him to do. But still, Moses had no idea how to free the slaves or how to lead them to Canaan. All he knew was that God wanted him to do it. So, he started; and he learned along the way. Mainstream churches and denominations need this kind of leadership. Leaders who have a center to their lives and know what mission they are on can give future-active leadership even if they do not have a road map.

Future-active pastors may not have a road map but they do take time to think and analyze. Today's pastor needs to spend at least five hours a week doing nothing but strategic planning—looking at people, things, and trends, and asking: "What does all this mean to this church in the future?" On many occasions Jesus withdrew from the crowds. We can say he did this to pray for divine guidance or to analyze the situation. But is there any real difference for the person whose entire life is based on a sense of mission to reconcile?

To have opportunities to think, these pastors prioritize how they spend their time. They cannot afford to be putting out fires all the time; nor can they afford to be anyone's personal chaplain. Churches need to staff sufficiently so that the pastor has this time. Otherwise, the pastor spends so much time putting out fires that he or she has no time to figure out how to prevent some of the fires.

During the 1970s and much of the 1980s, mainstream clergy who talked about evangelism were branded as mavericks. When they refused to waste time in denominational meetings and spent most of their time in the parish, they were considered loners. During these lonely times, they were sustained by their mission to reconcile. This subjective line of reasoning may sound like an excuse for bigotry to some. But throughout history, this call to reconcile has been the foundation for all spiritual leadership. No evidence suggests this has changed.

Pastors should not worry so much about whether or not people like them. They should concern themselves with whether their ministries are reconciling people to God. If a pastor has a need to be needed, he or she should direct that need to God, not to people. Rather than being codependent on other people's needs, pastors should let God strengthen them and give them more than life takes from them.

III
ORGANIZING FOR MINISTRY

The greater the emphasis on empowering lay volunteers to make the critical decisions in administration, the more likely that it (the local church) will be a small congregation averaging fewer than two hundred at worship.

Lyle Schaller

A changing, diverse world of choices demands a streamlined organization that emphasizes performance rather than coordination. The evidence suggests that Baby Boomers will not promote, protect, and subsidize the classic organizational structures denominations recommend for local church at the expense of ministry to people. Multi-layered bureaucracies, and democratic process do not allow for open, fast, flexible, decisive, and innovative ministry. For Joe/Josephine the days of going to endless meetings are over. Max/Maxine still see *meetings* as the primary focus for church leaders and members; but Joe/Josephine participate in churches where *ministry* is the major focus.

Denominational and local church structures in place before 1980 discourage ministry rather than facilitate it. Accountability is difficult and decisions are delayed because there are too many rules to follow and forms to fill out. Do away with as much structure and as many meetings as possible. Keep only the basic essentials. Establish priorities. Make everything flexible. Be conscious of time. Share information. Avoid hierarchical structures. Build in accountability.

Three guidelines determine the relevancy of local church structure: (1) major decisions can be made within sixty days, and most decisions can be made within one to two weeks; (2) the structure ensures that laity are responsible for implementing most of the ministry; and (3) information can flow easily in and out of the core leadership.

Figure 2 outlines a structure that meets these requirements. This structure emphasizes action rather than coordination—meeting the needs of people rather than maintaining the institution. Various forms of this structure are found in many growing congregations.

Figure 2

Move laity out of meetings into ministry. Joe/Josephine do not find fulfillment serving on committees; neither do committees develop leaders who understand ministry. Advent Church, located in Eagan, Minnesota, is filled with Joe/Josephines. Of their 351 members, 270 were born between 1946 and 1964. Advent has grown from an average worship attendance of 110 to 173 during the past year. According to the pastor, Loren Nelson, "These folks love going to a homeless shelter to prepare and serve a meal. They do not like to sit in meetings to plan a ministry to homeless people."

Many mainstream Protestants have the misconception that going to meetings is involvement in ministry and that holding an office is *the* primary form of discipleship. Holding an office in the church and going to meetings is not ministry. Important—yes; ministry—no. This spiritual domestication of the laity is ending. Joe/Josephine believe that God calls laity to something more important than keeping the church doors open.

The less laity are involved in the day-to-day administration of the church and the more they are involved in ministering to people, the healthier the church. Endless, boring committee meetings dwarf the power of the laity. Laity blossom when they minister to people; they wilt when they go to meetings. By the time meetings are over the laity do not have enough time or energy to be in ministry to people. Healthy, growing churches have a few paid and unpaid staff giving direction to the church so that the majority of laity are free to do the ministry of the church. The clergy, paid staff, and a small core of lay leaders sniff out the future, diagnose the present, and develop strategies and structures that move the people of God into the future through ministries that meet the needs of people.

The Church of the Servant in Oklahoma City was started in 1968. By 1987, it had 3,400 members with 1,650 people in worship. The church has an Administrative Council of 14 people, a Charge Conference of 50 people, and 1,400 people involved in specific lay ministries that are managed by objectives. The pastor, Norman Neaves, says, "What we have done is whittle our machinery down to as simple a function as possible on behalf of releasing laity for ministry."[1]

According to Tom Magee, the Executive Director of the Church of the Servant, the Administrative Council consists of the Chairs of Administrative Council, Finance, Pastor-Parish Relations, Trustees, seven members at large, the Executive Director, Senior Minister, and Director of Finance. Each member of the Administrative Council is a liaison with a staff member and works with him or her in their specific area. The congregation develops a Five Year Plan for all areas of ministry; then, the Administrative Council and staff develop the ministries to reach the objectives of the Five Year Plan. This plan is approved by the Charge Conference. From this point the staff works with the plan to ensure that the congregational goals are reached. The only people officially nominated are the Chairs of the committees, the Trustees, Pastor-Parish Committee, and Charge Conference. The staff chooses the "management team" to carry out the ministries.

Max/Maxine hate this structure for two reasons: (1) they equate Christian ministry with "running the church"; and (2) it threatens their control of the church. They are into power rather than ministry.

This structure frees the laity to do what they do best— share their divergent gifts and stories with others. It also encourages a more expansive view of lay ministry. Every aspect of life is viewed as ministry. Laity celebrate their gifts as salespeople, accountants, doctors, and truck drivers. As Stanley Menking, director of Continuing Education at Perkins School of Theology, says, "The church is not the focus of the ministry of the laity. It is a resource for ministry. The commitment made at baptism is not that we will be members of the church, but we will be agents for God's kingdom in the world."[2]

Establish a small executive committee and have as few standing committees as possible. The best way to kill a new idea is to give it to a standing committee. Standing committees tend to stress maintenance rather than ministry and often veto or delay new ministries. The Trustee committee is a good example. Money in the bank is guarded rather than used for ministry. The primary mission becomes making "their" money grow. Many Trustees see their role as protectors of the property rather than as a responsibility for providing facilities usable for ministry to people.

A small committee of less than fifteen people fosters the most results. It is much harder for Super Max/Maxine to dominate well-chosen small groups than large groups. Large groups are easily controlled by one or two strong-willed, vocal persons who passionately take a stand against change.

This executive committee performs several functions: it is a strategic planning group that designs ministries that benefit the entire church; it acts as a funnel through which ideas and concepts flow from the entire church; it is small enough for thoughtful and decisive consideration of the issues; it is difficult for any one person to dominate; and it speeds up the process of doing the work of ministry to people. This is the only committee anyone goes through to get approval by the official decision-making body of the church. Financial matters do not go through a Finance Committee. Nor do property matters go through the Trustees. If these committees still exist, they merely carry out the wishes of the executive committee.

Joe/Josephine should make up at least half of this committee. Be sure they are mature enough to participate in church politics. Do not put new Christians on small committees with Super Max/Maxine. They have a tendency to quit, and Super Max/Maxine then conclude that Joe/Josephine are not as committed as their generation. Joe/Josephine could care less about serving on a committee with Super Max/Maxine. They are searching for more substance to their lives, not more power.

Ministry teams are better than committees. Ministry teams have defined goals and they disband once the task is completed (task force is another term for ministry team). People know what is expected of them and have some idea of the duration of the commitment. Ministry teams are commissioned by the executive committee or nominating committee throughout the year as new ministries are started. This flexibility allows for quicker involvement of the laity. Joe/Josephine are far more mobile than Max/Maxine and need to be able to move into leadership roles within a few months of joining the church. Ministry teams provide that possibility; committees do not.

Nominating committees nominate only the chairperson of each ministry team and allow those individuals to choose their own teams. Such delegation of authority expands the number and variety of lay leadership. The result is a stronger and much more diverse lay leadership.

Rotate leadership every three years. Make every effort to involve new members in major leadership roles. Some churches have a yearly goal of new members comprising one-fourth to one-half of the leadership. Many churches stagnate simply because the leadership is stale and has veto power on all new ideas.

Build the organization around the flow of information. Today, information is power; it is also the foundation of trust. Joe/Josephine expect a free exchange of information. Hierarchical organizations do not interest them. They desire a partnership between paid and unpaid staff. They want to be consulted. Surprises upset them.

Performance, not coordination, is the goal of organizations that care about people. Meetings are not always necessary to share information. Use the weekly newsletter and worship bulletin. Conduct brief surveys or opinion polls at worship. Do in-depth surveys with the official body of your church. Provide easily accessible financial statements. Send out agendas prior to all meetings. Conduct "town meetings" where no vote is held to discuss major issues. Train leaders to listen to members and guests.

—————IV—————
TAKING AIM AT THE BABY BOOMER

*The real story of American religion is about . . .
aging donors, declining revenues, market share,
and a changing market.*

American Demographics 1988

No one comes to church by accident.

Friar Tuck

Healthy churches focus ministry on the needs of the unchurched as much as the needs of their members. Ninety-three million people in America reflect the values of Joe/Josephine. Three out of five are open to an invitation to attend worship. Mainstream churches grow when they intentionally reach out to this group and warmly welcome them into the family of faith.

Mainstream churches are dying because they focus primarily on themselves. Vacation Bible School is one of many examples. Vacation Bible School's original purpose was to reach unchurched children. Over time, mainstream churches institutionalized this ministry until it is now little more than a summer baby-sitting service for churched children.

Mainstream churches attract and assimilate Joe/ Josephine in three ways: (1) advertising that is directed at one of their specific needs; (2) invitations to attend church by a friend; and (3) ministries that meet their needs long enough to win them to Jesus Christ. This chapter explores the basics of advertising and personal invitations and lays the foundation for the people-centered ministries described in Chapter five (programs are referred to as ministries).

Advertising

Joe/Josephine respond differently to advertising than their parents. They prefer detailed information explaining why it is in their best interests to attend your church. Glossy photographs and clever headlines are not adequate anymore. Joe/Josephine want specific, documented, and informative material. Quality must characterize every facet of advertising.

Reaching out to Joe/Josephine is the first step in winning them to Christ. Two factors make advertising a necessity today (it was not a necessity in Max/Maxine's day): (1) People no longer attend church because of guilt, or parents, or peer pressure. People attend church today only because they want to. (2) Joe/Josephine either grew up in mainstream churches that did not meet their needs as children, or they did not grow up in a church. Their only idea of what a church can offer them is based either on their childhood experiences or on what they see on television— neither of which bears much resemblance to what vital mainstream churches are offering today. Growing churches tell Joe/Josephine why it is in their best interests to attend church.

Demographic studies help churches determine which ministries to strengthen or initiate. Church leaders think they know their community, but very often their perceptions are incorrect. In one large, strong church in Florida, 90 percent of the worshiping congregation was over fifty years of age. When asked why young people were not in worship, the members replied, "We are a retirement community." When they called the Chamber of Commerce to test their assumption about the community, they were surprised to learn that 60 percent of the community was now under fifty years of age. Since all of their ministries were for older adults, young people were not joining their church. They instituted more youthful ministries, and the worship attendance and offerings jumped dramatically the first year.

Two demographic tools provide the information churches need before starting new ministries. (1) Church Information and Development Services (CIDS) produces a demographic package designed especially for local churches.[1] The package includes growth/decline projections, color-coded maps, life-style profiles of the area, and a guide explaining how to use the data. (2) *American Demographics* is a monthly magazine that contains the most recent marketing information.[2]

Mass marketing no longer yields the best results. Marketing experts recognize between twenty-five and fifty different life-styles in America, and each one requires a different slant on advertising and promotion.

Direct mail, telemarketing, and radio are good ways to target a chosen audience. Direct mail is productive if used four to six times with the same mailing list—preferably concerning the same issue or ministry. CIDS provides mailing labels broken down into any chosen life-style. Telemarketing is very effective when used to plant a new church or ministry or to discover people's interests and needs. One hundred people calling five hours can dial ten thousand homes and ask three questions. Ten thousand calls results in a mailing list of seven hundred families. Criss-cross directories provide phone numbers by zip code.[3]

Build an unchurched file that is one-half the size of the membership. Provide a method of recording the name, telephone number, and address of every guest who comes to *any* event on your church property. Take special care to do this at events that involve large numbers of people from the community, such as arts and crafts festivals, auctions, or community dinners. Provide a door prize when registration is impossible. People give their name, address, and telephone number to be eligible for the prize. Follow up on these people, add them to your newsletter list for three months, and contact them by phone. After the contact, remove from the mailing list those attending another church.

Other ways to build the mailing list include asking members to provide names of friends they want to see attend their church and alerting the church when new people move into the community. Many cities provide a list of newcomers. The Chamber of Commerce provides the names and addresses of people making plans to move to your area.

Personal Invitations

The vast majority of adults attend worship the first time because they are invited by a friend, relative, associate, or neighbor. Studies done by the Gallup organization indicate that the majority of mainstream members are willing to invite others to worship—if they are motivated and shown how.

Business cards are good icebreakers. One fast-growing, Baby Boomer church in South Bend, Indiana, provides each member and constituent with five "Life-style evangelism cards." These brightly colored, easily read cards are shared with neighbors, coworkers, relatives, and friends. The cards contain the times of the services and a map showing the location of the church. According to the pastor, John Myers, "The cards work."

Bring a Friend Sunday. Many churches designate two Sundays a year as the time to encourage members to invite a friend to church. Four to six weeks of promotion precede the Sunday. Publicity includes information in the newsletter and bulletin, posters, and a special mailing. Members of the evangelism task force visit the Sunday school classes to inform them about the event. Several Sundays in advance the pastor preaches on the importance of the personal invitation. Extra greeters are provided for the special Sunday. A reception with refreshments is held after each service. An intensive, organized follow-up is provided within twenty-four hours. Several versions of this program are available.[4]

Aldersgate Sunday. Once a year, one church in Houston, Texas, celebrates Aldersgate Sunday. After adequate promotion, members are asked during worship to join the Aldersgate Club by agreeing to: (1) invite or bring one person to church during the coming year and help nurture that person into membership or discipleship; (2) attend a one-hour training session; (3) attend one celebrative event at the conclusion of the year; and (4) pray for each person involved in the ministry.

The goal of Aldersgate Sunday is to raise the visibility of evangelism and involve a large cross section of the congregation in becoming comfortable inviting their friends, relatives, neighbors, and associates to worship. Monthly reminders to the congregation appear in the newsletter and bulletin throughout the year. Every three months some form of reminder and encouragement is sent to each member of the Aldersgate Club.

Work your turf. Several churches use this popular phrase to encourage congregations to warmly welcome guests. From the time members get out of their cars, anyone that gets within ten feet of them is on their turf—and the members are responsible for them. Once a month the phrase "Are you working your turf?" appears in the Sunday bulletin. At every board meeting someone is responsible for reminding the leaders of their responsibility to work their turf.

Congregations work their turf best if their leaders are called hosts instead of greeters and new people are treated as guests rather than visitors. Greeters simply greet; hosts make sure their guests are comfortable and feel at home. Hosts assume responsibility for their guests throughout the entire Sunday morning experience. They may even invite their guests to dinner after worship.

Faith sharing events. Joe/Josephine are willing to talk about their faith if shown how. Growing churches provide events that teach them how to: (1) share their faith in natural, relational ways; and (2) become open and sensitive to the windows of opportunities provided by others who are looking for more meaning in their lives; and (3) proclaim Christ in ways faithful to the Scriptures and compatible with the times. Three resources are available for mainstream Protestants: a workbook and video presentation by Eddie Fox and George Morris entitled, *Faith Sharing,* a book by Eddie Fox and George Morris entitled *Let the Redeemed of the Lord SAY SO!,* and a workbook on faith sharing by Billy Abraham.[5]

Where Do We Start?

Three resources are available to help churches in the initial stages of planning ministries to Joe/Josephine: *Reaching for the Baby Boomers* is a workbook that suggests six guidelines for developing young adult ministries: (1) open wide the doors of the church; (2) provide basic "how to" handles; (3) provide stability and connectedness; (4) explore alternatives; (5) work short-term; and (6) provide a complete and high-quality package. [6]

A second valuable source is *U.S. Lifestyles and Mainstream Churches,* by Tex Sample. The author claims that the church needs ministries that: (1) are intrinsically valuable; (2) are emotionally expressive rather than boring; (3) develop deep and lasting relationships; (4) provide community outreach opportunities and address existing social needs; and (5) are unambiguous about the diversity of the Baby Boomer.[7]

A third source of information, *100 Predictions for the Baby Boom,* is helpful in planning ministries for the next decade.[8]

Begin evaluating the ministries of your church by asking five questions: (1) Are most of our major ministries conducted on the church property? Cooperative ministries, where several churches join together to carry out a ministry, benefit only the church where the ministry is held. These ministries are valuable to those individuals participating, but they do nothing for the health of the congregation. Participate in joint ventures only when it is necessary for that particular ministry to survive.

(2) Does the church provide ministries that reach out into the community and provide visibility for the church? These ministries meet a need of the community, and they keep the name of the church visible in the community. They usually do not have any direct benefit to the church. Meals on Wheels is an example.

(3) Does the church provide ministries that nurture and assimilate those who respond to the church's outreach? Adding people to the rolls of the church is not enough; assimilation into the life of the congregation is essential. Small group ministries and mission projects are examples.

(4) Does the church provide ministries that make disciples out of those involved in the life of the church? Being involved is not enough; people need a personal relationship with Christ and a knowledge of the Scriptures. Disciple, Trinity, and Bethel Bible Study are examples. [9]

(5) Do all the ministries of the church consider the needs of the unchurched and provide ways to establish a relationship with them? Healthy congregations seldom provide ministries solely for themselves. They know that churches are best nurtured by nurturing others.

View every ministry to Joe/Josephine as a means to an end. Meeting Joe/Josephine's needs is only the first step in the process of winning Joe/Josephine to Jesus Christ. Ministries are needed that help them make a commitment to Jesus Christ, join the church, and have the assurance that they belong to the family of God.

The weekday preschool or kindergarten is a good example of this process. Baby-sitting or renting facilities for others to use to care for children is not the role of the church.

However, growing churches use these services to introduce children and their parents to the Christian faith. Weekday child care is a means to an end—winning the children and the parents to Jesus Christ. The mission is reconciling them to God, not providing child care. Growing churches teach Judeo-Christian values in their weekday child-care ministry. They are up front and honest and advertise as church-sponsored Christian child care.

Before starting new ministries, expand, strengthen, and advertise ministries that are presently attracting Joe/Josephine. The most often underdeveloped existing ministry is weekday child care. Many churches have a one-or two-day Mother's Day Out that enjoys a good reputation in the community and has a waiting list. Expand it to five days and tell the community about it. The time, energy, and money to obtain a license are eminently worthwhile.

Start new ministries in anticipation of Joe/Josephine attending the church. When the suggestion is made to clean up and expand the nursery, Max/Maxine often respond, "Why should we fix up the nursery when there aren't any babies in our church?" Babies are absent in mainstream churches because of the deplorable condition of most nurseries. Fix up the nursery before Joe/Josephine arrive, not after. Otherwise, they visit and never return. The same is true about other ministries, such as those for singles, youth, and persons with handicapping conditions.

Start new ministries from the outside in. The pastor of Willowcreek Community Church in South Barrington, Illinois, began his ministry fifteen years ago by going door to door asking one question: "Why don't you go to church?" From the answers, he designed a ministry. During my first year as pastor of Colonial Hills United Methodist Church, I knocked on 2,000 doors asking one question: "What do you need from the church that you aren't getting?"

Self-determination is important to Joe/Josephine. Always plan ministries in consultation with Joe/Josephine. Ask unchurched people under forty what ministries they need from your church. If your church does not have any-one under forty years old to consult, go outside the church and ask the unchurched or church members of a younger church, or ask a consultant. Ask the church secretary what nonmembers calling the church inquire about most frequently. Ask church staff to listen to what people talk about between Sunday school and worship, at recreation, and at work. Pastors can find insights for new ministries by visiting places not normally attended by good church members.

Many of these ideas are viewed by Max/Maxine as nonsense, too expensive, or excessively extravagant. So include one or two well-respected Max/Maxines in the consultative process, and the idea will receive a better hearing by the congregation.

The following chapter contains concrete examples of how growing congregations are meeting the needs of Joe/Josephine. If any show promise for your situation, use them. But before you do, tailor them to fit your needs.

V

FEEDING THE BABY BOOMER

The most exciting breakthrough of the 21st century will occur not because of technology but because of an expanding concept of what it means to be human.

Megatrends 2000

Churches that reach Joe/Josephine offer a balanced variety of strategically chosen ministries. The preceding chapters have provided the context for selecting these ministries. This chapter outlines strategic ministries that help mainstream churches attract and assimilate Joe/Josephine. These ministries are divided into four categories—Biblical Education, The Family, Life-style Ministries, and The Journey Inward.

Biblical Education

The decline of mainstream Protestant churches cannot be blamed solely on demographic changes and population shifts. The primary reason for the decline is Joe/Josephine's refusal to remain members when they become adults. Many Joe/Josephines are attending other churches. Every area of this country is dotted with large, new, independent churches made up of Max/Maxine's children. The children of Max/Maxine are not found in mainstream churches for two reasons: (1) they were never personally discipled or grounded in the faith; and (2) they were confirmed into the church rather than led to a personal relationship with Jesus Christ.

The secret to long-term success with Joe/Josephine is adult education that moves them from a program- or friendship-centered faith to a Christ-centered faith. They need anchoring in Christ, not in a ministry of the church. Otherwise, when their children leave home, or when the program that drew them to the church goes sour, they leave the church. One of the major challenges facing mainstream churches is moving Joe/Josephine away from preoccupation with self to a deep and fulfilling commitment to Jesus Christ.

Mainstream churches put too much emphasis on "joining the church," and "working in the church," and "making a commitment to the church." Asking for this kind of commitment betrays our bureaucratic, institutional, pharisaical, maintenance-oriented mentality. This emphasis has no meaning for Joe/Josephine. But they will respond to an emphasis that seeks to ground them in Christ through adult Bible study.

Joe/Josephine desire two things from Bible study: (1) they want to know what the Bible says rather than what the church says about the Bible; and (2) they want to know how the Bible has been helpful in the lives of people they respect. Effective, hands-on Bible studies for adults provide both.

Adult Bible studies. Joe/Josephine need several types of Bible classes. In addition to basic Bible information, they need Bible studies that: (1) center on the particular needs of Baby Boomers; (2) focus on less affluent Joe/Josephines earning less than $12,000 a year; (3) provide learning experiences for people who like to work with their hands; and (4) aim at the thirty-five and under crowd.

Often, these classes are offered on a six-week basis. Some classes can be held away from the church on Sunday morning. But every church needs adult Bible classes on Sunday morning. If your church does not have one, start one. If it has only one, start a second one, and so on. Design at least one of these classes with Joe/Josephine in mind.

Classes that offer small group interaction are more important than lecture classes. One church in Norfolk, Virginia, is comprised mainly of Joe/Josephines. Over the last eight years, its Sunday school grew from 300 to 2,100 even though the church is not located in an area where megachurches are prevalent. According to the pastor, adult Bible study is one of the reasons for this growth. They encourage fellowship by limiting class enrollment to thirty-five and by dividing each class along strict age groupings rather than by gender.

Disciple Bible Study is excellent for adults or students during the week. This thirty-four week program meets weekly for two hours. Each class is limited to twelve to fifteen people. Each session contains a short video presentation. The primary emphasis is on reading the Bible rather than hearing about the Bible. Participants read approximately one hour each day in preparation for the class. During the study, 60 percent of the Bible is read.[1]

Early morning Bible studies fill a need of the young professional. Men and women meet at a restaurant for food, fellowship, and a study led by one of the pastors and are gone by 7:30 A.M.

In order to give some guidance in Bible study, many growing churches are providing bookstores in the foyers of their churches. Windsor Village in Houston, Texas, is one of the fastest growing churches in United Methodism. In 1989, twelve hundred people were added to the membership of the church. A bookstore is located in the foyer.

Church-sponsored elementary schools. Mainstream churches should consider developing more Christian elementary schools. By the year 2000, three factors will influence many Baby Boomers to send their children to private schools: (1) the poor quality of our public school systems; (2) the rise of crime and the lack of discipline in public schools; and (3) the fact that Joe/Josephine are already accustomed to paying for private preschool and kindergarten. Care must be taken, however, not to start such a school without a sufficient amount of paid scholarships to ensure that the school does not become an affluent ghetto and that the children are exposed to a wide variety of social strata. These schools teach Christian values and help reinforce the family.

The Family

Although family is important to Joe/Josephine, the nature and structure of the family have changed. Individualism permeates every aspect of today's family. Family togetherness is important, but the individual's space is equally vital. Understanding this change and building ministries that address this change are fundamental to reaching Joe/Josephine.

Ministries to families with children and youth. The Princeton Religion Research Center asked unchurched Americans what would bring them back to church. Their cited responses ranked summer programs for children and youth number one.[2] This is not surprising, since most parents now work outside the home. During the school year, school-aged children are in school, but child care is needed in the summer. When a church conducts a quality summer program that lasts most of the day, how could it miss?

One church has summer camp on site for the entire season. A director is hired in April or May to run the program and recruit the volunteers—with the salary taken out of the tuition. Experiences are offered on and off the church campus. The first year the church conducted the camp for one week. Each year another week was added.

Another church provides four Summer Mini-Music Camps ranging from one to three days in length. The goal of these camps is to: (1) prepare a children's music selection for worship on the following Sunday; (2) introduce the music for a children's musical in the fall; and (3) offer children a variety of instrumental experiences. The camps are on weekdays because attendance is better than on Saturday.

Parents' Night Out is another popular new ministry. The church provides quality child care on Friday or Saturday evening, with professional sitters or preschool teachers. A director is hired and a modest fee is charged to cover expenses. (Do not attempt this ministry with volunteers or teenagers.) One church discovered that a significant number of parents returned for their children after an evening of drinking. Instead of canceling the program, the leaders decided to expand the ministry by including AA material with the registration and to inform all parents that the church would exercise the right to decide if it was safe to release the children to their parents.

A church in Marshalltown, Iowa, provides a "Dial-A-Children's Story." According to the pastor, children call a special number to receive a recorded story approximately three minutes in length. Volunteers prepare the stories. At the end of the story, the message invites the child to attend Sunday school or summer Bible school. The program is paid for through the sale of stock certificates that read "All dividends are paid in children's smiles." Since this ministry began in 1982, an average of one hundred children have called each week.

Single-parent families need special attention. One church provides single parents with a sticker for their car that allows them to park in special parking spaces next to the nursery.

Partnership ministries between the church and parents that foster religious training in the home. Families are no longer the primary source of the transmitting of values from one generation to another. Today, parents sandwich the transmitting of values in between driving the children to and from events. Grandparents are not close enough to be role models. Public schools spend much of their time keeping peace. Churches have children for time blocks that are too short to transmit values. Children therefore receive most of their values clarification from television, gangs, and peer groups.

Joe/Josephine are uncomfortable with the gap that exists between their values and their life-style. Churches can help them narrow this gap by: (1) providing values clarification courses that help Joe/Josephine reach a precise understanding of their values and how those values affect their families; (2) providing resources and opportunities that help families reclaim their role as the primary source for transmitting values from one generation to another; and (3) publicizing that their church cares about families.

The weekly newsletter of one church features a children's story designed to be used by the parents in teaching the Bible at home. The story is called "Once upon a time." Each week the pastor writes a children's story based on Sunday's Scripture and relates it to the children's time in church the previous Sunday. Parents are encouraged regularly to use the story with their children.

A growing small church in the northeast has a section in the worship bulletin called "Key Word." The children are asked to count how many times the key word appears in the sermon and turn the number in to the pastor. The names of those who counted correctly are printed in next week's newsletter. Another church provides cassette tapes that can be played while driving children to various destinations. Another church includes a weekly synopsis of the sermons and the children's story hour at worship in the newsletter, along with an object lesson. Parents can call a designated number and receive a brief explanation of the Scripture text. The children can call another designated number and hear a recorded story.

More and more individual churches are sponsoring large family events. Usually, these events run from Friday evening through Saturday evening or Sunday afternoon. Coping with stress is a favorite topic. Sessions are included for the entire family and for parents, children, and youth.

Meals are served. Look for ways that your church can help families transmit values.

Quality child care. Joe/Josephine need free quality child care for every event in the church. During worship or Sunday school, separate the children under two years of age into three rooms—Crib, Crawl, and Walk. Keep the nursery clean and uncluttered. Provide a brochure for parents, telling them how you clean the toys and when you change the sheets. Change the carpet anytime it has permanent stains of unmentionable origin. Have paid attendants wear smocks or uniforms. Signs should remind the attendants to wash their hands after changing diapers.

If your church provides quality child care, tell the community about it. Send a letter to the parents of all newborns in your area, telling them that your church is ready to help them rear their children. (Most newspapers report births.)

Infant yard signs are a winner. Parents are loaned large signs for their yards that read "It's a girl. Welcome to the newest member of First Church." The most popular sign is a large stork carrying an infant.

Relational youth ministries. Youth ministries are divided into two types—relational and programmatic. Programmatic youth ministries are focused on one or two charismatic individuals. The strength of the program is centered in these few individuals. When they leave, so does the strength of the program.

Relationships are the key to vital youth ministries. Programs simply support the development of healthy relationships between teenagers and Jesus Christ, between teenagers and adults, between teenagers and their peers. Relational youth ministries are accomplished through small groupings of youth based on age. Large gatherings are held periodically to attract new youth.

Three words describe relational youth ministries—acceptance, growth, practice: (1) Youth need a place where everyone is accepted no matter how different they are. In relational ministries the word "different" has no value applied to it. Judgments are left to God.

79

(2) High-quality growth experiences are essential. Instead of trying to compete with the mass media, use creative, proven methods of communication—such as art, music, dance, drama, role play. Whatever form you use, make it challenging.

(3) Teenagers need opportunities to put their faith into practice. They need to learn by doing. Overnight and week-long periods spent on buses and at work camps provide many opportunities for youth to learn about themselves and the world.

Youth are looking for spiritual direction and a place to be loved consistently. Relational youth ministries provide both, along with stability.

The summer slump. In many areas of the country, activities are curtailed or discontinued in the summer, and church attendance drops. Church leaders say they do this because fewer people attend during the summer. The reality is fewer people attend in the summer because services are cut back. Summer slumps are not experienced if ministries are expanded in the summer.

One church in Los Altos, California, decided to end the summer slump and made the following decisions: The senior pastor began vacationing in the winter months instead of the summer. The church promoted a comprehensive ministry called "Summerful 87" that contained five events. These five events are now permanent: a major event with dinner each Thursday, an all-church summer camp on site, Vacation Church School, a full choir for each service every Sunday, extravagances on the 4th of July and Labor Day, and two youth musicals. In addition, a variety of special opportunities and activities are provided—such as a Homeless Shelter, Leisure Time Ministry, and a Spiritual Life Retreat during the week led by the senior pastor. Each Sunday is filled with music, drama, and new experiences—such as Sermons in Word and Song, The Wizard of Oz, Fiddler on the Roof, Dixieland gospel service, visiting choirs, and old-time hymn-sings. August is now the third largest month of attendance in the year. The pastor adds, "And it's a lot of fun, too!"

A small congregation in south Texas turned the summer slump into a summer hump by promoting the theme "Be a Slump Buster." Specific worship attendance and giving goals are announced for the summer. A different special event is planned for each week. A special summer preaching series is announced. Extra children and adult programming are punctuated with a heavy emphasis on fun. The result is a 10 percent increase each year in the giving and attendance patterns.

Financial planning seminars. These seminars not only help Joe/Josephine with one of their weaker skills; they also provide a ministry outlet for professionals that is not geared toward the maintenance of the institution. Lawyers, accountants, insurance agents, and other professionals can use their skills to provide hands-on help for people.

Life-style Ministries

Lack of time dominates Joe/Josephine's life; they have so many options to choose from. Joe/Josephine are individuals who live their lives strictly as they choose. They are defined more by the choices they make than by the dominant culture in which they live or with whom they choose to socialize.[3]

Small group ministries. Small groups consist of fewer than forty people who meet on a regular basis to nurture significant relationships. One small group is needed for every ten or fifteen people at worship. Small group ministries center around a variety of life-style needs, such as: Divorce Recovery Workshops, Blended Families, Sandwich Families, AIDS, Gamblers Anonymous, Women Who Love Too Much, Women in the Marketplace, CEOs, Job Placement, Codependency, Compulsive Behavior, Abused Women/Men, Mom's Support Group, Parents Without Partners, Incest, Veterans, Overeaters Anonymous, Exercise Classes, Engaged Couples Classes, Young Fathers Support Group, Alcoholics and other Twelve-Step Programs, Depression, Working Couples, Parents of Emotionally Disturbed Children, Men With a Family, and Prophylactic Personalities. Desert Shield/Storm support groups were needed in 1990 to 1991. Look for life-styles that need the support of a small group.

Weekday ministries. Growing churches have more people on the church property during the week than on Sunday. One 2,600-member church in Nashville, Tennessee averages 1,500 in Sunday worship and 700 in small groups each night of the week. A variety of ministries account for this phenomenon—preschool, Bible study, neighborhood groups, senior citizens, and small group ministries.

Many growing churches have a major week-night event preceeded by a quality meal. This event effectively: (1) appreciates the time crunch of most Baby Boomers by consolidating meetings and making them shorter; (2) allows every member of the family to participate at the same time rather than at various times spread over the week; (3) facilitates coordination between committees; (4) produces excitement because of the critical mass of people; (5) makes meetings less dependent on clergy; and (6) gives children and youth an opportunity to be with their friends. (Large churches discover that even with this week-night event, other activities scheduled during the week are needed due to varying work shifts.)

The meal is from 5:30 to 7:00 P.M. followed by several options: (1) communion at 6:30 and being home by 7:15 P.M.; (2) staying for a Bible study, lecture series, parenting class, children's choir, or various meetings and being home by 8:00 P.M.; (3) or participating in an adult or youth choir and being home by 8:30 or 9:00 P.M. Parents can pick up their preschool children after work and go straight to church, because excellent child care is provided. The meal costs between $2.50 and $4.00. Food service costs are paid out of the price of the meal.

Catered meals. Because many two-wage-earner families eat most meals out or catered in, take-out food is one of America's fastest growing small businesses. Older Joe/Josephine's spend up to 34 percent of the family budget eating out. These factors suggest that quality, catered meals improve attendance at church functions. Many churches provide a Sunday breakfast, brunch, or lunch.

Workplace ministries. Much of Joe/Josephine's life revolves around the workplace: relationships are formed there; UPS delivers to the work address; and lunch is a time to shop and run errands. Organized lunch groups and fitness centers at the church are effective methods of addressing this situation.

A church in Seattle, Washington, promotes the Seattle Lunch Club. Members of the church invite people in their office building to meet over lunch for small group experiences once a week. Once a month, all the groups meet together in a hotel. The time consists of sharing in the thoughts of a respected business leader in the community, followed by small groups. This ministry results in many new first-time guests to the church.

Downtown churches effectively reach Joe/Josephine by providing fitness centers open to the public. These centers include weights, running tracks, treadmills, exercise programs, gymnastic equipment, showers, etc. In most cases these services are paid for by the public. Often, classes are offered in various gymnastics. Churches can offer the services much more reasonably than private business.

Hands-on, locally controlled missions. Denominations need to recognize the demand for more local control in selecting missions projects. The failure to act on this point will produce a denominational mission program decline during the early part of the twenty-first century, as more churches respond to Joe/Josephine's desire for self-determination and the denominationally loyal Max/Maxine pass from the scene. Joe/Josephine like to choose where their money goes and to participate personally in some form of hands-on missions on a short-term basis. Habitat for Humanity is a mission project that meets both these requirements. Joe/Josephine are open to involvement in a project like Habitat, especially if asked to build a specific house to support a specific family.

One church promotes "Vacations With a Purpose." Six or seven times a year a different team will go for ten days to places like Guatemala or Haiti. Half of the time is spent working in a mission field and half as vacation. Personal growth is the goal. Bible study and personal sharing are part of the experience. Upon returning home, many become far more involved in the ministry of the church.

Sport ministries. Athletic ministries are one of the top attractions for reaching and assimilating Joe/Josephine. Peninsula Covenant Church near San Jose, California has developed a remarkable athletic ministry. Several years ago they acquired adjacent property that included a clubhouse and a large swimming pool. Instead of doing away with the pool or simply using it for the church, they expanded the clubhouse, put in a pro shop for various sports, and opened the pool to the community on a paying basis. Even though no intentional effort is made to evangelize those who use the facilities, several families who are now active members first visited the church as a result of meeting church members at the pool.

One church developed an extensive athletic ministry that involves more than half of the worshiping congregation. Three of their key lay leaders joined through this ministry. Two were unchurched at the time they joined. In the spring, an athletic banquet is held to honor all the participants. The attendance at the banquet usually ranges between 150 and 200. Approximately 7 percent of the unchurched who participate in these athletic ministries eventually join the church. The lay person who coordinates the program supplies the names of those who are not members of the church to the evangelism committee, which then follows up on them. Co-ed sports are essential.

Transitional ministries. Much of Joe/Josephine's life is spent transitioning in and out of short sections in their life cycle. Very few follow the life-cycle pattern of their parents—leave their parents to get married and or go to school; live with one spouse; have children and watch them grow up in their home; become empty nesters; one spouse dies and the survivor lives alone. This disruption of the normal life cycle is caused by cohabitation, delayed childbirth, divorce and remarriage. Most cohabitation arrangements last less than two years. Most marriages last an average of four years. Even the traditional nuclear family lasts less than seven years. Joe/Josephine live alone less than five years. And single-parent families last less than four years before remarriage or the children are on their own. Transition is the name of the game for Joe/Josephine.

People are more responsive to an invitation to attend church during these periods of transition in their life cycle, especially if support groups are available to meet their particular need. Divorce recovery workshops are one of the most commonly observed examples of these transitional ministries.

High-tech opportunities. Ten- to twelve-minute video tapes depicting the various ministries of the church and introducing key leaders are proving to be effective tools for relating to Baby Boomer visitors. The video provides two natural points of contact with the family—when it is delivered and when it is returned.

Computers in the Sunday school are helpful in giving children an incentive to learn Scripture. Studies show that many young children have more trouble reading a book than they have working a computer. A variety of software is available for Christian education, ranging from those that only require answering questions, to programs that allow the children to develop their own designs or material. Software is also available for non-reading first-graders. Most computer stores have catalogs from which to order Bible software. Some of the more popular software programs are Books of the Bible, Bible Baseball, and Noah's Ark.

One church has a children's computer room available on Sunday morning. Each children's class uses the computers about every other month. The crossword puzzle in Figure 3 was created by a fourth grade class. The children worked in teams to create it, using the Beatitudes as the source material. During Vacation Bible School, a fifth grade class produced a newsletter describing the events of the week.

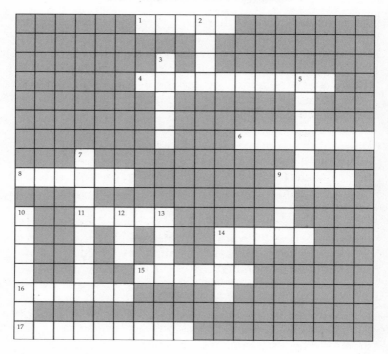

ACROSS CLUES

1. A holy book
4. Matthew 5:3-12
6. The first book in the New Testament
8. A place to worship God
9. Talk to God
11. A messenger of God
14. To be sad
15. A place where God is
16. We worship God, Jesus, and the Holy_____
17. Followers of Jesus

DOWN CLUES

2. Preparation for Easter
3. Our Savior
5. When Jesus rose from the dead
7. Someone who teaches about God
9. Not rich in God
10. In God's favor
12. Antonym of the devil
13. To have a special liking
14. Quiet

Figure 3

Importance of television. Over the next few decades people will "read" more books on video rather than read them in print. Our world seems to be increasingly dominated by sights and sounds rather than print. In time, even sound may give way to almost total visual reception of knowledge. The eye is becoming far more important than the ear. If it cannot be seen and felt, it will not be received. The more a church uses television, the healthier the church will be.

Large churches, in particular, need television ministries as an outreach to shut-ins and hospital patients. But in addition to that obvious need, large churches need television in order to attract and retain Joe/Josephine as active members. This technology is one of the most powerful tools in the history of education, and has become the symbol of a church that is interested in communicating with this generation.

Lyle Schaller said his "greatest single mistake over the past three decades has been to underestimate the power of television." He said:

> Television not only has transformed the habits and value systems of most Americans, it has also had a profound impact on the rearing of the children, on people's expectations of anyone who seeks to communicate with them, on the design and organization of the sermon, on the enlistment of new members, on funerals, on youth ministries, on Christian Education, on church schedules, on the criteria for congregational self-evaluation, on our language, on replacing regional cultures with a national television culture, on American foreign policy, on speech patterns, and on how people receive the news of the world. [4]

Women's ministry. In their book, *Megatrends 2000*, John Naisbitt and Patricia Aburdene list "The Decade of Women in Leadership" as one of the ten megatrends for the 1990s.[5] Josephine is not like her mother. Intelligent modern women are searching for a healthy balance between home and work demands, a balance that is elusive and precarious. Traditional women's groups do not meet their needs. Today's woman needs three things from the church: (1) practical "how to" seminars in balancing career and home, parenting, values clarification, support groups for mothers, and opportunities to come to terms with overcommitment; (2) powerful leadership roles that are challenging and give direction to the life of the church; and (3) schedules that take into account her very busy life. The more institutional and denominationally based the material used by the women's groups, the less likely the groups will grow and attract Josephine.

Quarterly Sunday school teachers. Many churches find it necessary to allow members to sign up to teach for three or four months instead of twelve. In reducing the commitment to a shorter period of time, an entirely new and larger group of teachers is attracted. Once they get their feet wet and realize how supportive the church is, people are more willing to teach longer or to sign up for a second term later in the year. Quarterly teachers create two problems which must be considered to ensure a quality program: continuity and training. Children prefer a familiar face, and quarterly teachers require quarterly training programs.

The Journey Inward

Public belief in and commitment to Jesus Christ is growing among Joe/Josephines. When asked why they returned to church, 67 percent of the unchurched said it was either because of an inner need to go back to church or to rediscover their religious faith. Another 18 percent said that it was because as they grew older they thought more about eternal life. Another 8 percent said it was because they had an important religious experience.[6] Baby Boomers are looking for churches that provide avenues for exploring the meaning of these experiences and how to incorporate them into their daily lives.

Retreat settings. Retreat settings produce more personal growth than do routine settings such as Sunday school. Churches need several retreats a year.

Several groups—such as The Walk to Emmaus and Chrysalis, the high school youth version— are some of the fastest growing spiritual renewal programs in the church today. These groups have intensive retreat settings for beginning members. The retreats strengthen and renew the faith of the members, and help them to get in touch with their feelings. Time is set aside for fellowship, study, prayer, and worship. The entire experience is bathed in a warm, loving atmosphere of acceptance in which participants can receive anew God's grace and grapple with the call to discipleship. After the intensive retreat experience, the participants are urged to continue meeting regularly with a small group of graduates. The purpose of the small groups is to encourage continued growth in grace and provide accountability for each person's decision to live a life of intentional discipleship.

This weekend may be the first time Joe/Josephine take adequate time to evaluate how they feel about their lives and about their relationship to God. Pastors need to provide follow up to shepherd participants and help them relate their renewed commitment to their own congregation.

Crises ministries. Joe/Josephine are extremely vulnerable when faced with crises. Their obsession with instant gratification does not serve them well when they are faced with advancing years or death, or a deformed child, or the loss of a job or spouse. They experience a high level of stress in all areas of their lives, and they do not grow old gracefully. As this group progresses in age, their need for coping and crises ministries will increase rather than decrease.

More people seek help when a certified and church-approved counselor is on the church staff. Large churches often provide free counselors on staff, while smaller churches allow qualified counselors to use their facilities free of charge in exchange for a specified number of counseling hours a week for church members. As more Joe/Josephines are reached by the church, more counseling is required.

The Stephen Ministry is an excellent way to develop trained, qualified lay counselors for a variety of needs, such as recovering alcoholics, recently divorced, persons contemplating suicide, chronically ill, unemployed, elderly shut-ins, and parents of new children. This ministry emphasizes support and does not disregard the need of professional help. Stephen ministers commit to give a minimum of one hour per week for two years.[7]

Relationship-building opportunities. Churches that reach Joe/Josephine in significant numbers provide numerous planned fellowship opportunities. Between 1971 and 1985, St. Luke's in downtown Jackson, Mississippi, experienced constant decline. By the early 1980s, the Sunday school had very few children and youth and no Sunday evening activities. The church decided to stop this decline and made an intentional effort to reach Joe/Josephine. A number of new ministries were started such as the Child Learning Center. Sunday school classes were looked upon as points of entry for new members. The nursery was redesigned, refurbished, and adequately staffed.

What really stands out about St. Luke's is their intentional commitment to providing diverse relationship-building opportunities for Joe/Josephine. They have several continuing week-night Bible studies, including one night with a catered meal designed primarily for Joe/Josephine. The puppet ministry is an outlet for Joe/Josephine's compassion and need to reach out to others. An annual Baby Boomer Shrimp Boil is held to which Baby Boomers invite their friends. The St. Luke's Softball Ministry was also started for Baby Boomers.

According to the pastor, "One of our chief Baby Boomer ministries is our Brad Gordon Memorial Mexico Dental Mission." This ministry was the dream of a Baby Boomer and has involved significant numbers of Baby Boomer professionals. Each year, the church takes a team of dental students, hygienists, dental assistants, and nutritionists to La Bartoline, Mexico. This ministry has spawned other mission groups to undertake construction projects and arts and crafts for the children. As a result of their efforts, one-third of the church is now under thirty-five years of age; children increased 200 percent; and worship and Sunday school are growing again.

A Baby Boomer church in Kansas discovered that drama provides a way to reach Joe/Josephine. In the past six years the church has produced and performed numerous plays and musicals to packed houses. Each endeavor involves an average of 150 people in the production, most of whom are Baby Boomers.

Church-wide prayer ministries. The organized use of intercessory prayer is one of today's essentials for reaching Joe/Josephine—as well as for helping them look beyond themselves to their neighbors. Various methods are used to encourage intercessory prayer at worship: (1) receptacles at the entrance to the sanctuary where people can place their prayer requests prior to the worship service; (2) collection of names during Sunday school; (3) listing of prayer concerns on the registration cards; and (4) a prayer "hot line" for people to call during the week and leave on a recorder the names of people in need of prayer on Sunday. Some churches have prayer teams that meet prior to the worship service to pray for the people worshiping. One church provides a twenty-four hour prayer vigil before every major all-church event. Another church prints in its Sunday bulletin the following: "If you would like to receive a prayer or special blessing this morning, a pastor will be available to you in the area between the pulpit and the piano after each service." Many churches establish elaborate prayer chains that extend throughout the church. [8]

Healing ministries. The need for acceptance and to belong, the fragmentation of society, the isolation caused by technology, the stress of our changing and complex lives—all of these can devastate the human spirit. As a result, healing ministries are growing in importance.

Two churches giving leadership in this area are Calvary Church in Colorado Springs, and Foundry Church in Washington. Both churches provide a formal weekly healing service. Adequate study and preparation preceded the development of the healing ministries in both congregations. From the start, the congregations understood that healing ministries never have a failure. Healing ministries are not evaluated by the amount of physical healing that occurs. Their primary concern is the wholeness of spirit, mind, body, and relationships. Healing ministries treat the person as a unit. If one's spirit is healed, the healing of the body is enhanced.

The healing ministry at Foundry Church includes study and meditation classes, intercessory prayer groups, personal counseling and visitation, special workshops and retreats. All of these ministries revolve around the weekly healing worship service. This service includes a meditation on a Scripture passage related to healing, and silence for prayer and meditation—with the main emphasis placed on Holy Communion and the laying on of hands. After the leaders lay hands on each other, they invite others to kneel and have hands laid on them. This is followed by silence and a brief prayer of thanksgiving.[9]

Calvary Church in Colorado Springs is an upscale professional congregation with 900 members, 600 of whom are in church each Sunday. The weekly healing ministry began in 1989. During its first year, over 40 percent of the entire worshiping community attended the healing service more than once. Twenty-five to thirty-five people attend each week. People attend the service when they feel a special need. According to the Minister of Programming, "This ministry has done more to heal the congregation than anything else in my eight years at Calvary."

This ministry includes a formal service that focuses on spiritual, mental, relational, and physical healing. Two lay persons assist the pastors in the service, which includes prayer, communion, and healing. Oil is placed on each person along with the laying on of hands. Leaders used two books in developing the ministry: *Blessed To Be A Blessing*,[10] and *Letters on the Healing Ministry*.[11]

During the 1990s, churches that reach out to Joe/Josephine will experiment with many new ministries. Some of these ministries will return to the basics of Christianity; some will be totally unrecognizable to people born before World War II. But all of these ministries will be strategically chosen to address the current needs of people rather than denominations. Those mainstream churches that develop a balanced variety of strategically chosen ministries will grow forward into the twenty-first century.

VI
GIVING IS LIVING

Do not lay up for yourselves treasures on earth,
where moth and rust consume and where thieves
break in and steal.

Matthew 6:19

You cannot serve God and mammon.

Matthew 6:24b

Churches that reach Joe/Josephine develop stewardship ministries that appeal to the human need to give rather
than the institution's need of money. The most effective
way to reach Joe/Josephine is through their compassion for
others and their need for meaning in life. They will not support a church budget or denomination out of duty. This
means that (1) churches can no longer rely on guilt or gim-
micks to raise money; and (2) denominations can no longer
expect congregations to blindly support the denomination.
Joe/Josephine are forcing the church to return to its basic
heritage of developing faithful stewards rather than merely
raising budgets.

Six factors are changing the way churches develop Joe/Josephine into stewards: Joe/Josephine's aversion to commitment; their passion for ecology; the volatility of world economics; the scarcity of discretionary income, along with the increase in accumulated income; shorter and more frequent vacations; and waiting longer to get married the first time and each time thereafter. Because of these changes, mainstream churches need: (1) a new theology of giving that emphasizes tithing in response to an inherent need to give; (2) targeted, short-term stewardship ministries; and (3) a more diverse leadership.

Churches that want to attract Joe/Josephine need a new theology of giving. A relevant theology of the stewardship of money for our time is a combination of Joe/Josephine's interest in ecology and the human need to give. The theme of this new theology is—LIVING IS GIVING; GIVING IS LIVING.

This theology acknowledges the fundamental relationship between divine creation and human fulfillment. God created all life and constantly shares with the creation all that God is and has. Everything we know about God confirms that God always gives us the best. God created Adam and Eve and gave them the Garden. Throughout the Old and New Testaments God gave many covenants to satisfy our spiritual needs. God so loved the world that God gave the greatest gift of all—Jesus Christ. Finally, God promises to give us a new heaven and a new earth. No one can read the Scriptures without realizing the giving nature of God.

Since we are created by a God who gives, we have an inherent need to give. It is as much a part of who we are as the need to be accepted, and the need to find meaning in life. We reach our potential by sharing life, not by hoarding it. Fulfillment in life is found as we express our God-given need to give of ourselves. Jesus said: "Whoever loses his life for my sake will find it (Matthew 16:25*b*)."

The fact that not all humans are aware of their divine need to give reveals the breach in the relationship between God and creation. Because of this separation, we do not know how to achieve the most out of life. We feel frustrated, and we do not know why. Joe/Josephine express this frustration when they say, "I'm not getting enough out of life," or "My faith isn't satisfying me," or "Isn't there more to life than this?", or "All the church does is ask for money." Many people are unhappy because they do not do what should come naturally—giving. Jesus addressed this need when he said, "It is more blessed to give than to receive (Acts 20:35b)."

The fulfillment of human nature comes through many forms of giving. One form is the giving of our financial resources. Joe/Josephine experience much of the fulfillment they seek when they become the master of their money. A contemporary, biblically-based theology of giving ensures that the goal of a church's stewardship of money is to develop sound teachings regarding *who* are in control of *what* God has given them. The goal is never simply to raise money.

The goal of this new theology is the tithe. I do not intend to argue the biblical case for the tithe. I believe in the tithe because of what I have seen it do in the lives of others and what it has done in my life. Tithers never seem to be unhappy or negative. They never complain that the church is always asking for money. People who tithe seem to have more, save more, and get more out of life than those who do not tithe. Tithers always seem to come out on top no matter what happens in life. Tithers learn how to prioritize their lives and resist the consumer orientation of our society. Tithers discover that fulfillment in life is found not in taking but in giving. Joe/Josephine need to discover how good it feels to be a tither.

John Maxwell, the pastor of a church in Lemon Grove, California, has developed a program called "God's Guarantee." Using Malachi 3:10 as the basis, he offers his congregation a ninety-day money-back guarantee to everyone who tries tithing and is dissatisfied with the experience. The results have been outstanding.[1] When people experience the joy and freedom of tithing, much more happens than increased offerings; their lives change.

Another program that stresses tithing and percentage giving is "Consecration Sunday," developed by Herb Miller. This program enjoys tremendous success in small to medium-sized churches. With slight modifications, it also works well in larger churches. A new edition of this ministry is being prepared just for larger churches.[2]

Targeted, short-term Stewardship ministries are essential to developing Joe/Josephine into stewards. Year-long, unified budgets will not develop as many Joe/Josephines into regular givers or tithers as a diversified set of opportunities. Joe/Josephine need some short-term opportunities to make commitments so they can evaluate the risk, get their feet wet, and grow into long-term commitments. Short-term commitments allow Joe/Josephine to grow in grace by discovering the incredible joy found in becoming good stewards of what God has given.

Churches are experimenting with stewardship programs that are six weeks to six months long. Some churches provide a core budget for staff and maintenance that is funded for one year, with many of the other items, such as buildings and missions, funded through special offerings throughout the year. Some churches update their pledges monthly; others give three-, six-, and twelve-month options on their pledge card. These churches have one major stewardship drive each year, with follow-up on those who choose to pledge on a shorter basis.

Churches using short-term pledge periods experience several advantages—an increase in giving, more pledges, a better percentage of payment, and more flexibility in the budgeting process.

One possibility is to conduct three mini-stewardship offerings for the budget each year—Christmas, Easter, and summer. Specific ministries within the budget can be designated to receive the funds from the offering. Some families will give more to the special budget appeals than to the regular budget.

Zero-based budgets are helpful. Zero-based means that each new financial period starts the budget process over from scratch, except for a few fixed items such as debt service. (It is best to include staff in the zero-base rather than the fixed items.) Every item has to be justified; otherwise, it is not included. Everyone agrees from the start that each pledge period begins a new budget.

Because a direct relationship exists between Joe/Josephine's worship attendance and their giving patterns, Joe/Josephine's tendency to take shorter and more frequent weekend vacations affects the way churches develop good stewards. Monthly contact, either by phone or mail, is needed with busy non-regular attenders. The communication should be detailed and honest, should describe how their money was spent, should stress how their giving made a difference in the lives of people, and should give recognition to the donor.

Because of the decline in discretionary income among young adults, encourage planned giving with emphasis on the goal of the donor. Rather than stress the *method* used for planned giving, stress the *benefit.* For example, if the method of planned giving is selling bonds to finance a building program, stress that the bonds can be put aside for the children's college education. The bonds are a donation to the church and the interest is tax free. Rather than stress how the bonds will help the church, stress how the bonds will help the Baby Boomers reach their goal of providing education for their children.

Some churches are promoting "Alternate Gift Certificates" for various celebrations such as Christmas, birthdays, anniversaries, etc. Instead of buying a gift for someone who may already have everything, the church provides an alternate gift. The donor makes a gift in honor of someone for use in some designated mission project, and the church sends the person an "Alternate Gift Certificate."

As bad as it sounds, it is time for the use of credit cards in church. One church in Arkansas used them for the first time in 1990. People stood in line at the end of the year to get all of their 1990 pledges in during the present pledge and tax year. Many of them could not have paid their pledges in full without the benefit of credit. Initially, most credit cards cost a church about 4 percent. But as the number of users goes up, the percentage charged to the church decreases. Bank drafts work also. Members sign a form that allows the bank to charge their account with the amount of the monthly pledge.

Once a month, one Baby Boomer church purchases equipment on consignment that it could not afford to purchase outright. The equipment is placed in the foyer with an attached price tag. Usually within two weeks, someone removes the price tag and makes a gift in the amount of the purchase.

Three leadership roles are required for developing an effective stewardship ministry: Spiritual Leader, Strategist, and Administrator. These three roles are filled by one or more people, depending on the size of the church. In well-staffed churches, these roles are clearly divided between two or three people. Understaffed churches either combine them or do not provide all three roles. Small churches seldom understand the need for these roles.

In order to discuss these roles, churches are divided into four categories based on average worship attendance—200 and under, 200-500, 500-900, 900 and over.

STEWARDSHIP ROLES

CHURCH SIZE	SPIRITUAL LEADERS	STRATEGIST	ADMINISTRATION
0-200	Pastor	Pastor	Pastor
200-500	Pastor	Pastor	?
500-900	Pastor	Pastor/Church Administrator	Church Administrator
900+	Pastor	Pastor/Church Administrator	Church Administrator

Figure 4

In every church, regardless of size, the role of spiritual leader is filled by the pastor. Pastors who understand that giving is living, approach stewardship as a vital way to help Joe/Josephine find the fulfillment they seek, rather than as a means to fund the church budget.

Pastors need to set an example of tithing by sharing with the congregation how much they give—either a dollar amount or a percentage amount. Joe/Josephine need to know how their pastor feels about tithing and how tithing can bring fulfillment, not only to those who receive, but also to those who give. Because Joe/Josephine give out of compassion, it is more meaningful for them to hear about their pastor's experiences than to hear a discourse on what the Bible says about giving.

The pulpit is a major avenue of spiritual leadership. One pastor of a large church was loaned a new car each year by a member of the church. The day came when the pastor lost the use of that car, leaving the family with one car. The pastor had a dilemma—does she buy a new car and cut her pledge, or does she buy a used car and keep her pledge? At the time, her pledge was approximately 22 percent of her salary. She decided to share this information with the congregation in a sermon on "Setting Priorities." She never told them what she was going to do about buying a car, but she asked them to watch how she dealt with her need for a car. Several weeks later, a key lay person pulled her aside and said, "I see you bought a used car. I guess I'll do the same." That person is becoming a steward of his money, because his pastor was the spiritual leader of the steward-ship of money campaign.

Pastors who understand that giving is living, encourage those who are obviously lagging behind in their giving level to consider the joy of giving. Spiritual leaders are not afraid to talk to members about being behind in their giv-ing, because they know those people are missing the joy of living. These pastors unashamedly preach on the subject of money and on what the love of money can do to the church, the individual, and the family.

If a church has money problems, it usually has a spiritual problem too. Joe/Josephine are not experiencing the joy of the abundant life because they have not become the master of their money. The pastor needs to hold the church accountable when it tries to take the easy way by raising money. Identifying money problems as spiritual problems promotes the kind of accountability that also tends to solve the money problems.

Depending on the size of the church, the pastor may fill one or both of the other two leadership roles. In most churches with less than 200 in worship, the pastor also fills the role of Strategist and Administrator. Churches between 200-500 in worship usually have some staff help with the Administrative role. Churches over 500 in worship need the added help of a Church Administrator. Even then, the pastor is still involved as Strategist. In churches with more than 900, the pastor does even more of the Strategist's role.

The Strategist's role in stewardship grows in importance as the world becomes more complex. The Strategist surveys the overall condition of the church and does at least six things. First, the Strategist selects and develops the program to meet the specific needs of the congregation. In making this decision, the strategist considers several factors:

• The type and age of the church. Congregations with an average age around forty need an emotional approach; older congregations may need more emphasis on commitment or a combination of the two approaches.

• The prevailing tax laws. Tax laws change each year. Although most changes do not affect the giving patterns of the average member, they often affect higher-income families. Starting the pledge period in April instead of in the fall allows high-income families to give their pledge for two years and apply it to one year for income tax purposes. This can mean substantial savings in taxes.

• The date and type of the last campaign. Very few methods work for more than three or four years without some renovation. The more frequently each stewardship emphasis occurs, the less written material is needed. Do not try to run simultaneous campaigns for operating budgets and capital fund expenditures. Smaller churches will be less concerned about this point.

• The ratio of pledges to membership. If the total number of pledges is less than one-half of the total number of church families, the method should concentrate heavily on the one-half not pledging.

• The average pledge and income. If the average pledge is less than $1,000 per worshiper, including children, the Strategist will need to look for new leadership and new methods.

• Who and how many are joining. Younger new members require more conservative methods, an emphasis on compassion, shorter commitments, and more opportunities to give to special ministries. The more new members a church has the more complex and intensive the method needs to be. A high percentage of professions of faith demands a year-round stewardship ministry.

• Where will the money go? Where and how the money is spent is the basis for Joe/Josephine's compassion. In churches with a lot of Joe/Josephines, the education prior to taking pledges must indicate precisely where the money will be spent. The budget does not have to be in concrete before the pledge period begins, but the pledge drive should give some indication of what will be done based upon how much is pledged.

Second, the Strategist develops a plan of rotation. Each year, a different segment of the congregation is targeted and encouraged to enhance its giving: those who never pledge but give; those who pledge under $500 a year; those who increased their giving last year but are not yet tithing; those who are tithing; and those who are large contributors.

Third, the Strategist chooses stewardship leaders to form the stewardship team. These team members are chosen on the basis of their willingness to give rather than on the level of their giving; integrity within the congregation; attendance at worship; depth of spiritual maturity; and representation of the entire congregation.

Fourth, the Strategist projects the actual needs for the coming year beginning with a zero-based budget. Everything from the previous year is forgotten except fixed items such as debt service. The needs and opportunities for the coming year are assessed and a working draft prepared— based upon the objectives for the coming year and next year's financial projections. Such planning ensures that ministries that do not fit into the overall objectives of the church are not funded and money is available for new ministries.

Fifth, the Strategist projects each quarter how the year will end unless action is taken. Kennon L. Callahan's suggestion is excellent.[3] Compute the three-year percentage average for each month of the year and compare it to the actual income as it relates to the amount needed for the budget to date. For example, over the last three years, January's income equaled 6.9 percent of the total yearly income, February's 7.3 percent, and March's 7.7 percent. This means that by the end of the first quarter the income should equal 21.9 percent of the budget for the coming year. If only 19.9 percent of the amount projected is received, the church is 2 percent short for the first quarter. If that amount is multiplied by four, the church will be 8 percent short by the end of year unless some action is taken. Of all the Strategist's responsibilities, this is the one most likely to be shared with or delegated to the Administrator.

Finally, the Strategist divides the congregation into four groups: the 20 percent who give no matter what; the 50 percent who give if others give; the 20 percent who give after everyone else gives; and the 10 percent who love to say no.

These four classifications are important for stewardship ministries that use the stairstep method. Instead of taking all the pledges at the same time, those who give no matter what are asked to give first and the total results are announced. Usually, this group includes staff and core leaders of the church. After this announcement, the second group is asked to give. They are more willing to do so, knowing that others have already pledged. Next, the minimally involved members of the church are asked to give.

Do not waste time with or feel bad about the 10 percent who love to say no.

The Administrator's role in stewardship is becoming more prominent as stewardship ministries become more diverse, complex, and short-term. Churches without paid administrators find it helpful to hire an administrative assistant for six to eight weeks to oversee the details of the stewardship program. The money spent is returned severalfold, due to the extra attention and professionalism given the program by this person.

The Administrator's role consists of the following (all require the use of a computer in churches over 150 in worship): (1) coordinate the entire ministry; (2) act as a clearing house for all volunteers; (3) supervise all publicity; (4) provide all necessary material in a timely fashion; (5) keep accurate records and follow up on each segment of the program; (6) send out monthly financial statements regarding the financial status of the church and ministries accomplished; (7) send monthly statements to each member with an appropriate personal message; (8) in the tenth month of the year, send a note to those who are too far behind in their pledge to catch up, giving them an opportunity to renew their pledge at a level they can meet with integrity, or to cancel and make a one-time donation; and (9) ensure that each family receives offering envelopes each month rather than receiving a year's supply all at once.

Stewardship of money does not just happen. It requires hard work and diligent planning. Emphasis needs to be placed on the need of the person to give rather than on the need of the institution. Churches that reach Joe/Josephine will stress compassion for others and will offer a variety of options to give.

—VII—
THE SUNDAY
MORNING EXPERIENCE

Americans are expressing an intensified search for meaning in life, deeper relationships, and authority.

George Gallup, 1990

Legitimate Christian preaching sooner or later proclaims the life, death, and resurrection of Jesus Christ. The interpretation of these events includes a call to self-denial, the lifelong process of growing in God's grace, and the celebration of new life in Christ. This Good News proclaims that when we learn to give life away, the abundant life in Christ begins to unfold. Based on what we know about Joe/Josephine's inclination to self-centeredness, how do we reach them through our preaching? Will not some parts of this Good News sound like bad news to Baby Boomers?

Preaching

The goal of preaching for Baby Boomers is not to make people feel good or to make them feel bad. The arrow of biblical preaching points toward one unchanging objective—helping people establish and develop a growing relationship with God, themselves, and their neighbor. Whatever the sermon subject, pastors do well to ask, "Will this message help the listeners strengthen their walk of faith at home, work, or play?" No formula can ensure perfection in a sermon, but the following list can be useful in crafting messages that help Joe/Josephine discover more of God's truth for their lives.

Preaching is not pontificating. Telling the eternal truth each week tempts a messenger to begin thinking that he or she is the truth rather than a communicator of the truth. This temptation is inherent in the very nature of the preaching task. We are likely to preach with power what we have experienced in our lives. Yet, we must maintain the humility to keep the container of our own experience, in which we carry truth, separate from the truth in that container. When we fail to maintain this distinction, Joe/Josephine will sense it instantly and look elsewhere for spiritual nourishment. Preaching to Joe/Josephine gets the best results when sermons come from someone who seems to be on a journey or quest, rather than from someone who seems to be handing out decrees. John the Baptist, who proclaimed Christ without pretending to be Christ, is a good model for this complex role.

Preaching with authority. A messenger is not the authority, but he or she has the authority inherent in the message conveyed. Ineffective preaching that fails to impart truth to its listeners does not work with this operative. Joe/Josephine are not interested in sermons that sound like reviews of the latest book the preacher has read.

This does not mean that pastors are not always growing in faith; it means that there is an overall consistency to their life. People are looking for stability in the midst of their journey—authority in the presence of the world's chaos.

Moses is a good example for this complex role. During the wilderness journey, he was not always sure how to get to Canaan, but he never gave up the vision that God would lead him there.

Do not attempt to straddle the fence on major life-style choices. Joe/Josephine are uncomfortable with the gap that exists between their values and their life-style. They are looking for guidance in clarifying what is important in their search for self-fulfillment. They want to know how others have used their faith to work through life's problems. Sermons should be clear and decisive. The listeners want to know how the pastor stands on the issue, not a bibliography of options. They will listen and respect the message, even if they do not agree, as long as the material is not presented as a decree. One way to accomplish this is with a style that says, "This is what works for me."

Adjust the style, not the message. The style is how the sermon is presented; the message is the substance. Style is never as important as the substance of the message, but style determines whether the message is heard. As pastors distinguish between the style and the message, they discover new ways to effectively present the gospel to Joe/Josephine without compromising it.

Use any style that is effective in getting the message across. Be willing to give up those sacred cow cultural styles, personal opinions, and denominational traditions that can get in the way of communicating the gospel. One good way to adjust the style is to make the biblical story as contemporary as possible without changing the substance. Sermon One at the end of this chapter is an example of this kind of preaching.

Video is becoming a major medium that can be used in a variety of ways to reinforce the spoken or sung word. Before the service begins, video can be used to show major events during the preceding week—such as new infants, couples celebrating major anniversaries, and new church members. During the service, video can show recent mission trips of church members, scenes depicting the Scripture that is being read, major points of the sermon as it unfolds, members in need of prayer, words to the hymns, and in some cases, all of the worship program. Some churches have even replaced the hymnal with video.

"But," someone may ask, "where do we cross the line between proclamation and entertainment?" That may be a good question for some independent congregations, but it is not a legitimate concern for most mainstream churches. Most mainstream worship services lean far more toward boredom than entertainment. Without compromising the gospel, we must do what is necessary to hold people's attention long enough for the Good News to grab hold of them and start them on their journey of faith.

Hold up a vision of how life works. Many good sermons hold up two visions: One vision says, "What can be is always more important than what is or what has been." People need avenues of hope and concrete ways of finding spiritual security. A sense of purpose for their lives needs to be part of this vision. The other vision says, "We can deny self without denying life." Preach self-denial, but never the denial of life. Life was sacred to Jesus; he demonstrated that life should be enjoyed. The skilled preacher finds ways to show how self-fulfillment is found through giving one's life away—without giving life itself away.

Trust your personality to shape the message. Few Joe/ Josephines join a church; most join a personality. They perceive truth through the personality of the preacher. The pastor's personality shapes his or her preaching. Pastors should be different. No two pastors deliver truth in the same way. Each pastor must trust his or her instincts. Worrying about becoming a personality is pointless. If a pastor serves one church for more than five years, then new members will transfer their allegiance from the pastor to the Body of Christ.

Apply the message in practical ways. Effective pastors replace "ought to" sermons with "how to" sermons. They show how to take what is said on Sunday and use it in hands-on ways Monday through Friday. In order to do this, pastors need a working knowledge of the business world and constant contact with what is going on in the lives of both the members and the unchurched.

Make it memorable. People do not remember entire sermons and multiple points. They remember memorable pieces of a sermon. A pastor can preach on the faithfulness of God—thoroughly explaining God's faithfulness by using biblical terms, yet not one person in the pew may remember a thing about God's faithfulness. But what if that pastor uses the imagery of "Faithfulness Is Like a Dog With a Bone," describing the tug-of-war that begins when you try to take a bone away from a dog? Or, the pastor might risk bringing a dog with a bone into the worship service and try to take the bone away from the dog. God is like that with us. Like the "Hound of Heaven," God never lets go of us. No matter where we go or what we do, God is right there with us. That is faithfulness.

Preach on issues that affect the congregation. Never allow a major issue facing the congregation to go unaddressed in sermon form. Share your position on the issue. Offer some solutions. Encourage the congregation to pray about the issue. Setting major contemporary concerns clearly and openly before the congregation and offering possible solutions is one of the pastor's critical roles.

Use personal illustrations. Joe/Josephine desire a personal relationship with the pastor. This can happen in the sermon. Sometimes, the sermon is the only way it can happen! Time restraints may make all other alternatives impossible. The larger the church, the more people are prone to establish personal, almost intimate, relationships with the pastor—even though the pastor may not even know their names. They want personal insights into your life. They want to know what you find helpful in your walk of faith. Personal illustrations can help that happen.

Preachers walk a fine line here. They should be vulnerable without grandstanding. They should avoid illustrations that constantly cast them in a hero's role. They should not, however, be afraid to let the people know how they find self-fulfillment through their faith. People need to see how the pastor deals with feelings such as doubt or fear. When my wife was diagnosed with cancer, I shared with the congregation how we dealt with our fear. If the pastor is honest without being ostentatious, people will gain valuable insights while feeling a closer bond with their pastor.

Stress global concern. Joe/Josephine travel more than any other generation. And they look at the total picture more than any other generation. Therefore, provincial preaching is not effective. Joe/Josephine need sermons that have a global orientation, rather than a national or regional view. They want to know that their pastor understands how the gospel addresses the needs of the entire planet.

Do not be afraid of emotion. Mainstream Protestant churches sometimes make the mistake of believing that people can think their way into Christianity. This is not always true. Many people respond to the gospel through their heart, not their head. Joe/Josephine are far more emotionally expressive than Max/Maxine. Establishing a meaningful relationship with God and the congregation is more important than the head content of that connection. In many growing churches, the worship experience is an emotional experience, more like an athletic event than a lecture series. The sermon evokes deep emotions, and the worship service allows those feelings to be freely expressed. Competent pastors find ways to reach the emotions without loss of integrity in biblical and theological content.

Storytelling is more important today than ever before. Good storytelling does two things: (1) it allows the story to be told in contemporary language; and (2) it involves the congregation in the story itself. The best storytelling weaves the audience in and out of the actual story, shifting from past to present. The listeners begin to feel as if they are actually part of the story. Sermon One, listed in this chapter, uses this method.

Dramatic monologues also share the gospel story in contemporary form. The pastor assumes the role of a Bible character and shares a one-sided conversation with an imaginary person. The pastor might assume the role of Pontius Pilate and reminisce with an old friend about the day he washed his hands of Jesus Christ. Or, the pastor might assume the role of Mary and recount her experience of finding Jesus' tomb empty. This type of sermon can take twice as long to prepare. It must be memorized and delivered almost verbatim in order to have meaning and impact.

Avoid technical words. Except for basic biblical words, avoid technical theological words that need elaborate explanations (unless your primary goal is to teach about that word). Instead, use familiar words. Go back over several of your recent sermons. Circle the words that are not readily understood by people on the street. Replace them with more familiar words that do not hurt the integrity of the sermon. If there is no way to avoid using words that the unchurched do not know, take time to explain them. But be brief in that explanation. Otherwise, you will break the flow of the message. Few people find reading a dictionary to be a fascinating exercise. Even less interesting is having someone read you a dictionary.

Well-structured sermons move people best. The sermon structure usually determines whether it can move the congregation from one stage of development to another. Everything in the message must help move the listeners toward taking some kind of action that changes or strengthens their lives. How the sermon is put together determines how effective the content moves the mind from "that's interesting" to "that is something I must do!"

Most of my sermons begin with a question designed to immediately hook the listeners and help them decide whether this message holds any promise for them. This opening also sets the stage for the conclusion. Depending on the type of sermon, I spend two or three minutes exploring the implications of the question. The conclusion of the sermon is often in the form of a question which calls for a specific response from the individual. The conclusion may run as long as two to five minutes.

The material in between the two questions includes the interpretation and application of the text. These are presented in ways that help the listener come to terms with the opening question. The development of the biblical text is sometimes done as a block and sometimes interwoven throughout the sermon.

The most important aspects of this middle section are the connecting pieces, which I memorize. How effectively these connecting pieces are used determines how effectively the listeners are moved from one point in life to another. Sermon One, later in this chapter, contains thirteen connecting pieces. Each one is in italics. The power of the sermon depends on the effective use of these thirteen pieces.

Sermons need not have a clear-cut beginning, middle, and end to effectively move Joe/Josephine from one point in life to another. Much of traditional sequential thinking is disappearing. Young people seldom finish what they start, nor do they do things in the same order as the last generation. Many families have television sets with four screens and watch more than one program at the same time. Using the remote control, viewers flip through the channels. People do not think from A to Z as much as they once did, and have become more comfortable with different styles of communicating ideas.

Be observant. An understanding of human nature is just as important to preaching as a knowledge of the Bible. Temper your theology with your sociological observations. The more pastors observe human nature, the better they understand the Bible. Read as much secular material as you do theology. Spend time with unchurched people to discover what concerns them most. An understanding of the pressures of the workplace helps pastors relate the Scriptures to the mundane experiences of Monday through Friday.

Train yourself to look for a sermon in everything. The best sermons are born, not in the office, but out in the world away from the church and other Christians. Observation is the key. Allow life to provide the material for your sermons. Take notes on observations that come to you in the car, at the movies, at dinner, at recreation, watching television, etc. Keep a note pad by your bed. When around strangers, initiate conversation. Work on several sermons at the same time. Have one big file on all the ideas you are working on, and every three months throw away the ideas that have not blossomed into sermons.

Before preaching a sermon, allow it to become part of your personal journey of faith. Discover real-life illustrations that help the congregation remember the message. Integrity is important to Joe/Josephine. They know when the speaker is personally involved in the message. Canned sermons and illustrations are not as meaningful as those born out of one's own experience.

An example of such an illustration is a dolphin story I told during a sermon on trust.

> Some friends and I were fishing many miles offshore when we hooked something very large. After stripping most of the line from our reel, the fish turned and came straight toward the boat. A few yards from the boat we realized that we had accidentally hooked Flipper! As the dolphin came closer, we discovered that there were actually two dolphins. At the boat, the companion dolphin frantically danced across the water, making that familiar clicking sound. The hooked dolphin came right up to the boat, opened its mouth, and allowed one of the men to reach into its mouth and remove the hook. Then the two dolphins raced around the boat two or three times and disappeared.
>
> If it had chosen to do so, the dolphin was big enough and fast enough to fight us a long time. But eventually the dolphin would have lost the fight, either by breaking the line and possibly getting tangled in it, or by becoming so tired after a long fight that it risked being eaten by a shark before regaining its strength. Instead, the dolphin came straight to the boat as if it knew we would let it go. All the way home I thought about how much trust that dolphin had placed in us. We could have shot it, or gaffed it. But somehow it knew that trusting was its best hope. What if we humans learned to have such trust in God? How our lives would change if we gave up fighting life's battles of doubt and fear, and learned to trust God instead.

Keep it simple. Develop one major point and examine it from several different perspectives, much like examining the many facets in a diamond. Provide insight on one well-developed idea rather than on several superficial ideas.

Develop a system. Many good methods exist for developing and delivering effective sermons. I intend to share one method that has served me well for a number of years. If it is helpful, use it. If not, find one that helps you and the congregation grow in faith and develop as human beings.

The sermon title and text are chosen well in advance of the week they are preached. During the early to middle part of the week, a couple of hours are spent examining the text and developing a simple outline based on the text. The sermon is then set aside for a day or two to allow for thought and prayer; enough distance from the message to be able to determine if it addresses the Monday-through-Friday needs of the laity, and time to look at life through the perspective of the message.

Toward the end of the week, the sermon is outlined in detail. Two questions control the outline: Can unchurched people and most children understand the message? Can the sermon be preached without notes?

Sunday morning from 6:00 to 8:00 A.M. is spent memorizing the outline and the important transitional pieces, and practicing the entire sermon. The sermon is then preached without notes or the benefit of a pulpit. I carry a Bible with me when I preach, and sometimes I attach the sermon outline to the Bible.

This process requires, on average, about six to eight hours of preparation a week. Of course, the sermon begins in idea form a month or so before it is preached, and illustrations are gathered over that period of time.

Preaching skills can be learned. My first sermon was a disaster. I tried four times to say the first paragraph, and when I could not, I sat down. That failure was one of the best things that ever happened to my ministry. It taught me that good preaching would not come easy for me. So, if preaching is not yet one of your best assets, take heart. The skill can be learned.

The Celebration Hour

New concepts and forms of worship are perhaps the most pronounced changes seen in churches reaching Joe/

Josephine. In almost every case, these churches think of the Sunday morning experience as a celebration—a celebration not just in theory, but in practice. Many churches will speak of the "Celebration Center" instead of the sanctuary and the "Celebration Service" instead of worship. For these churches, worship is more of a joyful celebration of God's goodness than a somber time of meditative reflection.

Meditation has been misunderstood. Meditation is a spiritual experience that is normally pursued at times other than in worship. Many mainstream churches construct worship to be somber, containing periods of meditation before and during the service. As people enter the sanctuary, ushers remind them to be quiet, because others are praying. Joe/Josephine tend to see worship as a corporate celebration—rather than a time for somber reflection. To most Joe/Josephines, worship focused on meditation is boring.

Max/Maxine generally desire reverence and a subdued worship atmosphere. But meditation and worship do not necessarily happen at the same time. Many people believe that meaningful meditation is a private matter that bears much fruit outside of worship. Jesus said, "When you pray, go into your room and shut the door and pray to your Father who is in secret" (Matthew 6:6a). Worship is meant to be a celebration, even during Lent.

God is the audience. In a celebration service, the responsibility of the worship leaders and members of the congregation is to direct their praise to God, not to the congregation. People are there to praise God—not just to receive spiritual food. For this reason, praise choruses are growing in acceptance in mainstream churches that reach Joe/Josephine. The entire service becomes an offering to God. Intercessory prayers are as much a way of thanking God for whatever the outcome as they are a way of asking for a change in people's condition. Music is a ministry that directs people to God, rather than a performance that shows off the choir. Preludes and postludes are for the benefit of helping people transition in and out of worship rather than performances to be heard. And professions of faith in God are more important than joining the church.

When worship is understood as an act of praise to God, people come to church for a different purpose. Rather than coming to church to "get their batteries charged," they come to give thanks to God. They understand that worship is to give rather than to receive. And of course, the result is exactly what Jesus said it would be. In giving themselves to God, God gives himself to them.

Methods of congregational participation are changing. Joe/Josephine participate in worship differently than Max/Maxine. Responsive readings or long recitations of printed material do not speak to their needs. Joe/Josephine tend to desire more spontaneous and emotional participation. They want to interact with the lives of others. Joe/Josephine often enjoy participating by clapping, giving and listening to personal testimonies, sharing their feelings, and singing, playing, and listening to contemporary music.

In many growing churches, clapping during worship is encouraged—because clapping is Joe/Josephine's way of expressing their joy. It is a modern way of saying "Amen." Max/Maxine usually dislike clapping. They do not see worship as the place where feelings are expressed. They view clapping as a response to a performance.

Joe and Josephine generally respond better to spiritual autobiographies than to rituals or creeds. They want to know how others have dealt with their problems. They want to hear how other people have come out on top. Personal testimonies or interviews can be included in the celebration. These are five-minute testimonies of what God has done in people's lives, and what it means to be involved in that particular church. The intent is not to gain more volunteers or to promote a program; the goal is to allow members to share their joy in being a Christian.

Emotion is a central part of the worship of God. Yet emotion seems to be missing from most mainstream churches. Why? Because we have placed far too much emphasis on knowing about God and the church rather than on helping people establish a relationship with God and others. Mainstream churches have stressed content rather than feeling, and have forgotten that faith is a process rather than a static position with God or our neighbor. Turning pilot training upside down, they emphasize knowing FAA rules instead of knowing how to fly. In so doing, they have quite naturally forgotten that a relationship with God is more important than membership in the church.

In most growing churches, the music is upbeat and contemporary. Many churches follow Charles Wesley's example and use contemporary music that is understood and enjoyed by the average person. Choral music is seldom rendered in a foreign language.

A relevant music ministry includes six important characteristics: (1) variety is essential; (2) quality is expected; (3) fast and exciting is better than slow and quiet; (4) English is preferable to any foreign language; (5) familiarity or ease of singing is of supreme importance; and (6) praise choruses are acceptable.

Mainstream church music is often one of the major obstacles for Joe/Josephine. It is too difficult, too classical, and too out-of-date for Joe/Josephine to sing or appreciate. Music needs to be designed as a ministry to the spiritual needs of the congregation rather than as a performance by trained musicians. Many trained musicians say they believe this, but in practice act as if they do not. They feel they have a duty to "educate" the congregation as to what is "good" music. They seldom consider contemporary Christian music to be "real" music.

Congregational members often fail to see the choir as a place to participate, because of the choir director's attitude or the type of music he or she may choose. If you want more participation by Joe/Josephine, sing more contemporary music. Announce special music events a month before practice is to begin, and invite the congregation to join the choir for the duration of the practice and presentation. Remember, Joe/Josephine make short-term commitments.

A variety of celebration options are provided each Sunday. Sunday morning at a typical growing mainstream church consists of two or three "Worship Celebrations,"

Children's Church, and perhaps two Sunday Schools. Each service contains a variety of different experiences—drama, interviews, testimonies, dance, and visual presentations. Often, each service offers a different style of worship. Some churches offer a choice in preachers. A variety of choirs, ensembles, and solos are present in each service.

The opportunity to join the church is offered regularly, without compromising commitment to Christ. Joe/Josephine respond to the emotional impulse of the moment far more than do Max/Maxine. Joe/Josephine are not "joiners." If they are welcomed into the church as their need arises, and worked with closely, over time a larger and more faithful congregation is developed. Unfortunately, many churches still expect Joe/Josephine to wait for membership classes, which are held at the convenience of the church. All forms of church membership need to start where Joe/Josephine are and allow them to respond quickly to the emotions experienced in worship.

Three methods for receiving new members address Joe/Josephine's need to have an immediate response to the gospel and not to compromise commitment to Christ. (1) The Church of the Servant in Oklahoma City, Oklahoma, has monthly membership classes. At the end of the classes, the people join the church—right then. The next Sunday, at the end of each service, instead of coming to the front to join, the new members are welcomed where they sit. This allows them to remain with their families and friends. Those who are to be baptized or given the vows of Profession of Faith remain after the service for a special service of commitment for them and for their friends and relatives.

(2) Calvary Church in Colorado Springs, Colorado, also requires pre-membership classes. They offer classes every two months and are considering having them more frequently. They create a list of potential members and send them a letter telling them about the upcoming class. Follow-up phone calls are made to ensure attendance. Every Sunday, the Sunday worship program tells when the next class begins and how to enroll in it. Two choices are offered: a three-week, one-hour class, or a one-time, three-

hour seminar on Saturday. With a membership of 900, Calvary averages 600 in worship.

Churches that require these pre-membership classes need to do three things: (a) on a regular basis announce in the Sunday worship program the procedure for joining the church or professing faith in Christ; (b) offer the classes as often as is necessary; and (c) build the curriculum around developing a personal faith in God, finding a place to serve Christ within God's world, and appreciating the uniqueness of the local congregation. Remember that the perpetuation of the institution is never the goal of Christian education for Joe/Josephine.

(3) At Frazer Memorial Church in Montgomery, Alabama, membership training takes place after joining the church. People are encouraged to join weekly but then are required to participate in a membership class to help them find a place of service in one of Frazer's many ministries. Every Sunday the following invitation is extended to those participating: "If you have made any decision this day or this past week that you would like to share publicly with this community of faith, or if you would like to join this church either by transferring your membership or by making a public confession of faith, you are invited to come forward during the invitational hymn." The statistics at Frazer are impressive. Even though they define an inactive member as one who has missed three weeks consecutively, only 11.6 percent of the membership is considered inactive.

Our church allows people to join each Sunday and does not require membership classes before or after joining. Instead, we build in intentional ways in which assimilation and growth occur. Each week, our staff monitors each new member on the anniversary of his or her first, second, and third month as a member. A trained team of laity go into their homes the first month to help new members decide where they wish to invest their time in ministry and to answer any questions about the pledge card. By the end of the ninety days we hope to have them involved in worship 75 percent of the time, a Sunday school class or weekday Bible study, a volunteer ministry of the church, and the stewardship of their money. Using this method, 87 percent of our new members are active in these areas as they begin their second year of membership, and our average worship attendance ranges between 46 to 49 percent of the membership, which is high for a congregation of this size. In 1991, we began requiring a one-hour orientation session after joining. This is offered monthly. The goal is to receive their pledge, and time and talent commitment.

The Sunday worship program is designed with Joe/Josephine in mind. One Sunday an affluent young attorney, who had never been to church before in his life, walked out of our church and asked one of the staff, "What was that the congregation mumbled during Mass?"

He was referring to the Lord's Prayer. He not only did not know the difference between Mass and Protestant worship; he did not know the Lord's Prayer well enough to recognize it when he heard it. Now, we print the words to all of the pieces of worship—such as the Doxology, the Lord's Prayer, the Gloria Patri, and the Affirmation of faith. More and more people attending church are like this young attorney.

Because Joe/Josephine are not traditional "joiners," it may prove beneficial for the worship program to talk about "belonging" to the church family instead of joining. A copy of the back page of a sample worship program is provided in the appendix.

Informality is stressed. From praise choruses to rituals, churches that are reaching Joe/Josephine put a premium on informality. The Church of the Servant mentioned above does not have a visual focal point for the Celebration Service. The choir sits as a group in the congregation without robes. They sing and return to their seats. The robed clergy are scattered throughout the congregation and do their part in the service—such as reading scriptures or welcoming the new members—from various microphones located within the congregation.

More and more churches allow the choir to sit in the congregation. This gives them the freedom to be part of the music ministry and sit with families. By the end of this decade many mainstream pastors may discontinue wearing robes because of Joe/Josephine's dislike for institutions and formality.

The attitude and wholeness of the pastor is central to the relevancy of the preaching and the worship service. Pastors who relate well to Joe/Josephine have most of the following characteristics:

They have a curiosity about how life works. Life is viewed as a learning experience. They view their own life and spiritual development as a process that is always changing and in need of exploration. The gems they discover are passed on to the congregation, not as absolute truths, but as personal observations about how life works for them. Their sermons show that they are open to and comfortable with change.

They have a compassion for people's relationship with Jesus Christ. Their goal in preaching is not just to make people feel good but to direct them to examine how they relate to Christ. They are passionate about ministry and view it from a life-and-death perspective. Ministry is not just one way to live life; it is the only way to live. These pastors have those same high expectations for every member of the congregation.

They have the courage of their convictions. The congregation knows by listening to their sermons that they have a very clear sense of personal direction. The congregation senses that even though their pastors are searching with them, there is a purpose and direction to their search. This purpose and direction shines through every message. They speak with authority.

Sermon Examples

Sermon One

This sermon, "Does God Really Love Rascals?," explores the results of immediate gratification. It was preached after a counseling session with a young man who had just been unfaithful to his wife, was going through bankruptcy, and was facing an audit by the IRS. The important transitional pieces are in italics. The text for the sermon is Luke 15:11-24.

Does God really love me, even when I'm unlovable? Have you ever made a big enough mess of your life that you asked this question? Given the circumstances, you're not sure if God really still loves you.

Jesus must have dealt with this question many times in his ministry, because over and over he answered it in one way or another. On one occasion, he said, "I came not to call the righteous but sinners to repentance." On another occasion, he said, "Those who are whole do not need a physician like me." But of all the times he tried to answer this question, none is so marvelous or so comprehensive as when he shared with us the misnamed parable of the Prodigal Son. I call it the misnamed parable because I think that this is not a parable about a prodigal son, but one about a father who loved his son even when that son was unlovable. *As we look at this story, we're going to find that this could be our story, and as such, it answers the question, does God love me even when I am unlovable?*

Our story has two characters: the father, who represents God; and the son, who represents you and me. The story opens with the son deciding that the time has come for him to have everything that belongs to him. He doesn't want to wait until his father dies; he wants to have all of his inheritance right now, so that he can enjoy life while he's still young. He knows that it is his right by Jewish law to ask for his inheritance whenever he chooses. So, he goes to his father and says, "Dad, I want what's mine and I want it NOW. It belongs to me. I want to go and spend it as I choose."

The young man embarked early on a life of taking rather than giving. And in the background we hear the echo of the words of Jesus, "Those who lose their life, find it. Those who save their life, lose it."

A lot of people today are like this young man: presuming upon the Father's good nature; taking the Father for granted; assuming that at our every point of need God will be there to give us whatever rightfully belongs to us. We set out to satisfy immediately all of the needs that we can possibly satisfy. We yearn for immediate gratification, and we go through life taking and never giving anything back. We become takers, rather than givers. We work hard to save our life for self rather than spend it on others. We delude ourselves into thinking that we are such special people that we focus all our energies on ourselves. *And by doing so we set ourselves up for failure.*

And that's exactly what happened to the young man. He failed miserably. He went out into the far country, as far away from God as he could get, and he squandered his money in "loose living." The phrase, "loose living," is painfully familiar to many of us.

The young man squandered everything that he had. He had a great time for awhile. He satisfied every immediate need that he had. And then the Bible says that when he got to the end of the rope of immediate gratification, he began to realize that it wasn't enough.

Over these twenty-one years that we have been together as pastor and people, I have watched numerous families climb the corporate ladder and begin to spend more and more on themselves—buying bigger houses, bigger cars, more vacations, better vacations, and better clothes. They charge their credit cards to the maximum to accumulate things and gratify immediate needs. I've watched these good families stretch the rope of immediate gratification until it finally snapped and they cried out, "Is that all there is to life? There must be more!"

It's no coincidence that Harold Kushner's little book, *When All You've Ever Wanted Isn't Enough,* is a best seller. So many of us are living examples of the story of the prodigal son. We don't want to wait until tomorrow; we want it, and we want it now. *And the more we want the hungrier we get.*

The young man in our story was so hungry that he was willing to sell anything that he had to get more. He was so hungry that he was willing to sell out his own value system. And that's what he did. He sold himself as a slave to do the one thing that no good kosher Hebrew would do. He not only fed the pigs, he lived with them. He sold out his whole value system. The young man sank deeper and deeper until he reached the very bottom of the barrel.

Anytime we sell out our basic value system, anytime we become a slave to anything or anyone other than God, we begin the long, painful descent to the bottom of life's barrel. We may have the world's goods lying at our feet at the moment, but the time comes when we are compelled to ask, "Is that all there is? Isn't there more?" And the day comes when we recognize that the view at the very bottom of life's barrel is not a very scenic picture.

But from the very bottom of the barrel, the Bible says the young man "came to his senses." He looked at the way things were. He examined his life. "What have I got to show for my inheritance? I've wasted it all. Even the hired servants at home live better than I do. They have a better relationship with my father than I do. Maybe I should go home. Maybe I should re-establish some kind of relationship with my father and take whatever he gives me. Maybe a life of service to him with nothing is better than bean pods here with all the pigs. I'm going home, and if need be, I'll spend the rest of my life as a servant of my father."

It's at this point that you and I determine whether or not we ever get an answer to our question, "Does God love me even when I am unlovable?" What do we do after we satisfy all of our needs and it isn't enough? What do we do after we have tried our best to give our children everything we didn't have, and it isn't enough? What do we do after we jump through all the hoops and do everything the world says we should do, and it isn't enough? If we come to our senses and realize that life with God with nothing is better than life with the pigs with something hollow, then and only then are we able to begin to get an answer to our question: "Does God really love me even when I am unlovable?" What we do at this point determines our future.

What did the young man do? He did a 180 degree turnaround. He left that country and returned to live with his father. He made his way home. And as he turned down the little path that led to the front door of his home, he saw his father standing at the front gate of the house, with the gate swung wide open. Upon seeing each other, they ran to each other and embraced; and the father kissed his son. The young man was finally at home.

The father told the servants to bring the fatted calf, his ring and robe, symbols of all his remaining wealth, and he gave them to his son. For that which was lost is found and that which was dead is now alive. Can you feel the arms of the father embracing his son? *Wouldn't you like the Father to welcome you home in the same way?*

Does God love us when we're unlovable? You bet God does. God loves us even when we deliberately squander all our inheritance on loose living. God loves us even if we sell ourselves into slavery and destroy our value systems. No matter what, God still loves us.

But our story has one tiny catch. If we stay in the far country, we never get the answer to our question. We hear that God loves us. He's standing at the open gate, waiting to accept us; but if we stay in the far country, we'll never personally know the answer to our question. We can wallow around in self-pity, asking, "Why me? Why doesn't life work any better? Why has life fallen apart?" We can wallow around in our self-pity out in the far country and never know that God loves us. We'll never know, unless we leave the far country and make our way, as painful as it might be, back to the place where God is waiting for us.

Can you feel the arms of God around you? Sure you can. Are you ready to make that one-hundred-and-eighty-degree turn and come home to God?

How do you come home to God? Just like the young man in our story did. Ask God to forgive you and take you back.

Why not do it right now? You can trust God to accept you just like you are. *For God loves even a rascal like you.*

Sermon Two

This sermon, "Mountaintop Experiences," was preached the Sunday after Nelson Mandela was released from prison. It shows how self-fulfillment is found in self-denial. The text is Matthew 17:1-8.

Have you ever had a mountaintop experience that tremendously affected your life but over time faded away to the point that you sit in church wondering if it ever happened? Have you ever wished that you could sustain those high and holy moments and make them last forever?

The scripture text we read a moment ago is going to address this desire. It shows us how our mountaintop experiences can be translated as sources of daily strength.

Theologians call this text "the Transfiguration." It's a very difficult text to translate into our lives. A good way to help us understand the implications of this text for our lives is to do two things. First, we can familiarize ourselves with the events before the text and what happened after it. Second, we need to read behind the lines, because a whole day's events are abbreviated into nine short verses.

So, I'm going to retell this story, using modern language. It might prove helpful if you follow the story in your Bibles. As I tell the story, listen very carefully, and you just might hear God sharing with you how you can take those marvelously wonderful, wild, and sometimes wacky mountaintop experiences that come so seldom, and make them part of your everyday life.

One morning, Jesus decided that he wanted to go on a picnic. The day before had been very rough, and he needed some R&R. He had a great need to get away and think.

He got out his picnic basket and began to fill it for the picnic. First, he got his sodium-free salt. Next, he spread low cholesterol veggies between two pieces of whole wheat bread, wrapped the sandwich in a biodegradable napkin, and put it in the picnic basket. Finally, he got a blanket, some napkins, a stainless steel knife and fork, jumped into his Honda, and off he went to Peter's house to see if he would go with him.

On his way to Peter's house, Jesus reminisced about the rough day before. Just a few hours earlier, Jesus had shocked his friends by telling them that soon he was going to die for the sins of the world. He had never told them that before. Peter was so disturbed that he grabbed Jesus and shook him and said, "No! I won't let that happen!" Overlooking Peter's impulsiveness, Jesus rebuked Peter, saying, "Get behind me, Satan." He would have given anything to take those words back. "How could I say such a thing to my best friend. I'm supposed to be the Son of God!" And his doubts about himself began to mount.

As he knocked on Peter's door, his concern over re-establishing a relationship with Peter intensified to the point that he prayed, "I hope he isn't home." But Peter was at home. Jesus asked, "Pete, how about going on a picnic with me? We need some quality time together to sort things out." "You mean you're still speaking to me?" Peter replied. "Why, I thought I was the devil himself!"

And Jesus said, "Pete, let's go re-establish our trust in one another."

Peter's eyes lit up. He raced to the kitchen, found his picnic basket, got out his Twinkies, salted pretzels, and chocolate chip cookies. Next, he wrapped his greasy brisket in aluminum foil—along with his plastic knife and fork and plastic foam cups—put them in the basket, and off they went.

On the way, Peter suggested that they invite James and John to go with them—because they too were upset by the day before. "You know how sensitive John is," Peter said. "He was very disturbed by what you said to me." So they stopped by the home of James and John. They agreed to go, and the four of them jumped into John's Suburban and off they went to the mountains for a picnic.

As they made their way up the mountain, Jesus remembered the expression on John's face the day before. John's spirit was crushed when he heard Jesus say, "I'm going to die for you, John." But his spirit had fallen even more when he heard his role model call Peter, "Satan." John still appeared to be a bit shaken from the experience the day before.

When they got to the top of the mountain, they found a beautiful spot to spread out their picnic blankets. They put their food out and began to eat. They had a marvelous time of fellowship, in spite of the ubiquitous ants.

Suddenly, two big UFOs began to hover overhead. Jesus' appearance dramatically changed. He became iridescent, and the disciples were dumb struck. They began to hallucinate and heard the strangest things—Moses and Elijah appeared and conversed with Jesus. Suddenly, they heard the voice of God: "This is my beloved son. Listen to him." Wow! You know it is a mountaintop experience if God speaks. You can't get more spiritual than that!

All of the traditional trappings of great religious symbolism were there—a mountain, a shining garment, a shadowy cloud, and the Law and the Prophets. It was a great, marvelous morning for Peter, James, and John, and especially for Jesus. All doubts about Jesus' identity were over. Not only did he know who he really was, but so did Peter, James, and John. He had received divine confirmation about his role as the Messiah, but this experience firmly established his unique relationship with God. Now, Peter understood the words Jesus had spoken to him the night before.

Everyone in this room has had a moving religious experience of some kind. I'll never forget the night outside of Bertram Air Force Base in Austin, Texas, in a tent revival. I was a young man of sixteen, listening to a hellfire and damnation preacher. The night was bitter cold outside and not much warmer inside the tent. That night, for the first time in my life, I heard the voice of God. I heard it as audibly as Jesus, Peter, James, and John heard it. The voice was real. God said: "I want you. No ifs, ands, or buts about it." All my life, when I have come up against life's difficult, terrible, dark moments, I go back to that event and find my grounding for life. I'll never forget it. You've had them too—those events that you always go back to when life gets tough.

Peter, James, and John never forgot that day. It was a vision of what life could be, and they would go back to that event time and again when faced with doubts and difficulties. Just like you and I do.

It was Peter who spoke first. It was always Peter who spoke first. He's a lot like you and me. The Bible says that Peter, not knowing what to do, spoke before he thought. "Lord, what a morning! Why don't we build three sacred cows and live here forever!"

That's about the dumbest thing Peter ever said. It was so dumb that Jesus didn't even respond to it. He just began to gather up all his stuff. The disciples followed suit, shaking the ants off their goodies and packing their bags. Down the mountain they went. Down from the mountaintop, down from the glory, down from the wonder, down to the valley of human hopes and hurts and despair.

All the way down the mountain, Jesus talked to them about what it meant to die on behalf of others. He talked about everything being in place now and how it was time for him to go to Jerusalem. "I'm ready," he said. "I have heard God speak. I know what I've got to do, and I want you to understand why." All the way down the mountain he told them what it meant to live life on behalf of others.

Folks, very little of life happens on the mountaintop. Those "experience highs" are short-lived and intense. But real, joyful, fulfilling life is lived on the way down the mountain. As we take the mountaintop experience down to where God's people are—that is where the real living goes on.

The problem with many of us is that we spend too much of life trying to climb up the mountain. We expend so much of our energy climbing the ladder of success—crawling over one body after the other—so we can get up to the pinnacle of achievement. And have you noticed how brief is the feeling of being on top? Mountaintop beliefs never last nearly as long as we anticipate. And the higher we get, the harder and more painfully we fall.

The rewards of the Christian life are not found at the top of the ladder of success. The abundance of the Christian life is experienced by applying our brief mountaintop encounters to help other people have some of those same wonderful moments.

When Jesus and the disciples reached the bottom of the mountain, they were greeted by an epileptic boy. The Bible says he was so filled with seizures that they thought he was possessed with a demon. As far as the disciples knew, it might be the same demon that Jesus cast out of Peter the day before. They didn't know anything about epileptics. All they knew was that the boy was filled with demons.

As Jesus approached him, the epileptic boy stretched out his hand to Jesus and cried, "Lord, help me. Your friends have tried to cure me, but they can't. Can you help me, Lord?" The disciples told Jesus that it was useless to try to help. They knew all the reasons why nothing would work. But Jesus ignored them, reached out, grabbed the epileptic by the hand and pulled him to his breast, and healed him. He does the same for you and me every time we are seized by the demons of greed, apathy, jealousy, pride, or bigotry. Whenever the quality of our lives is threatened, he pulls us to himself, and he heals us.

The great theologian, Augustine, compared the world to a chicken with its head cut off—flopping around on the ground spewing blood everywhere. Have any of you ever rung the neck of a chicken? If so, you know the mess it makes. Augustine said the world needs someone to put its head back on it. Like the boy with epilepsy, the world is wrenching in pain and is in need of someone to ease that pain.

The real living of life is done in the midst of helping others. Not on the mountaintop, but down in the valley. Jesus spent his entire life going from one mountaintop after the other down into the valley of human need. And now he says to us, "Go, do likewise."

If you want to know how to live out your life in ways that give meaning and self-fulfillment, then translate your mountaintop experiences into the lives of other people, so that they can know the joy of living life to the fullest. By doing so you will relive the experience yourself. But if you attempt to keep life's mountaintop experiences to yourself, they will fade and flicker, and someday be only a distant memory. And you'll wonder why you don't get more out of your faith than you do. Reach out to this hurting world and embrace it in your love.

This last week was one of those mountaintop experiences for many people. For years, many of us have prayed for the release of Nelson Mandela. What a glorious sight it was to see the day when Mandela was freed from prison. Even though I spoke about his release last week in worship, it's still difficult for me to talk about. Few events have had such an impact on my life. His release was a mountaintop experience.

But you know what? Mandela's freedom is not worth a thing if every day of his life Mandela isn't willing to stand before the threat of an assassin's bullet and fight for the total freedom of blacks in South Africa. Unless he continues to be willing to give his life on behalf of others, he will never find meaning and fulfillment in life.

That's what Jesus tried to explain to his friends. "Those who give life, find it; those who try to preserve it for themselves, lose it." Nelson Mandela understands that. He has been to the mountaintop. Can you imagine the ecstasy he must have felt as he stood on the courthouse steps a free man after twenty-five years in prison? But he knows that the fulfillment he felt that glorious day isn't worth a thing unless he is willing to brave the assassin's bullet for the rest of his life. That's the gospel. Those who lose life, find it!

What are you willing to give in order to find what you are searching for? What valley of human need must you descend to in order for those few high and holy moments in your life to find daily expressions? Don't try to find life by keeping it to yourself. Learn to give it away. Learn to live for others, for by doing so you find life.

A FINAL WORD

Those churches wishing to implement the ideas contained in this book will do well to do the following:

First, identify the Super Max/Maxines and the bridge builders. Convert or isolate Super Max/Maxine to the point that they can no longer stand in the way of progress. Nurture and equip the bridge builders to be effective bridges between Max/Maxine and Joe/Josephine. They will need constant encouragement in the face of the inevitable conflict.

Next, identify those future-active leaders who have the ability to look into the future and embrace change, diversity, and a wide range of choices. Place these leaders into all the key elected offices, with the very talented comprising the executive committee.

Third, streamline the organizational structure around ministry rather than maintenance. Emphasize performance rather than coordination. Allow for quick decisions, and design the structure so that information can flow freely in and out of the core leadership.

Fourth, focus at least half of the ministry on the needs of the unchurched. Develop creative ways to reach out to Joe/Josephine and tell them why they will benefit your church. Be clear who your unchurched audience is and train the members how to share their faith.

Fifth, develop a balanced variety of carefully chosen ministries centered around biblical education, the family, lifestyle ministries, and the resurgence of spirituality. Included in these new ministries will be creative new ways to develop tithers. At the same time continue to effectively nurture Max/Maxine through more conventional ministries.

Sixth, design worship to be celebrative and informal. Stress contemporary music and when possible, use visuals. The more practical the experience, the better. Many churches will find it necessary to start additional worship services in order to implement this kind of worship experience. This way, Max/Maxine are not offended.

Remember, it will not matter how carefully these suggestions are implemented—Super Max/Maxine will be upset, and a few Max/Maxines will feel ignored or forgotten. But those who are committed to Christ rather than to the institution will be on board and ready to lose their lives in order that others may live.

APPENDIX

SAMPLE SUNDAY SCHOOL
TEACHER/CHURCH COVENANT

Christian education is the barometer for the long-term health of both the individual and the church. We should, therefore, expect nothing from ourselves and of our church other than our "committed best."

The goal of every teacher in our Sunday school is to provide a relational atmosphere in which each student and teacher grows in her or his relationship with and understanding of God, neighbor, and self.

Because of the tremendous importance we place on the Christian education of our children, students, and adults we covenant to do the following:

I. I,_____as teacher of _____class, agree to give my "committed best" from the period of_____to_____in doing the following:

1. Strive to keep a personal attitude of willingness to share myself and the Bible with the students entrusted to my care.
2. Be in my classroom no later than 15 minutes before class is scheduled to begin, prepared to teach.
3. Seek inspiration and growth both for myself and those I teach through the Teacher Training workshops.
4. In the case of absence, notify my team teacher by the Wednesday before the Sunday class (unavoidable absences, such as illness and emergencies are exceptions).
5. If my team teacher is unable to teach, I will notify a substitute (from my list) or a parent of my need.
6. Shepherd my students by contacting those who are absent each week.
7. Attend worship on a regular basis, so that my example may be a role model to others.

II. We, the church staff and lay leaders, agree to give our "committed best" to support the Sunday school teachers by providing the following:

1. Upholding them in our daily prayer life.
2. Whole-family participation in Christian education and encouragement of parents' involvement in their children's classes.
3. Curriculum, resources, and supplies.
4. Teacher orientation and training.
5. Quarterly planning/training workshops.
6. Continual evaluation of current Christian education programs, seeking out and supporting new ideas.
7. Creative and innovative materials that help further Christian education.
8. A clean, well-lit, furnished room.

Agreed to and approved this_____day of_____19___

Teacher	Minister of Education
Dept. Coordinator	Pastor
Dept. Coordinator	Pastor

SAMPLE MUSIC MINISTRY
MISSION STATEMENT

Our Vision for Music Ministry

To provide the wide variety of quality music that is achieved when all three major choirs average one person in the choir for every 10 people in the congregation.

Our Strategy for Reaching This Vision

OBJECTIVE ONE: To identity, recruit, train, lead, and deploy 150 lay people into ministry. The music ministry is a ministry rather than a performance.

OBJECTIVE TWO: To coordinate and implement four special choir events a year—including cantatas for Easter, Summer, Christmas, and the Pops Concert.

OBJECTIVE THREE: To coordinate and implement the following special services—Maundy Thursday, Christ Child, Christmas Eve services, which includes a children's musical.

OBJECTIVE FOUR: To provide once-a-month strings and/or brass accompaniment, and by the end of 1992 to have our own instrumentalists from the church.

OBJECTIVE FIVE: Along with the Senior Associate, plan and coordinate the music and service of worship.

OBJECTIVE SIX: Along with staff, plan and implement one major extravaganza each year that becomes a tradition.

OBJECTIVE SEVEN: Coordinate, plan, and supervise the Youth Choir Tour each summer, including fund-raising and planning the itinerary.

OBJECTIVE EIGHT: Provide quality music for Vacation Bible School.

OBJECTIVE NINE: To be provided by the Director of Music and Fine Arts. This can be up to 10 percent of the job description.

The above objectives are considered essential to this position and the Director of Music and Fine Arts is evaluated in the light of each objective. Each of the objectives is open to negotiation.

Other Expectations, Responsibilities, and Information

1. It is understood that there can be no more than one classical piece a month, never in Latin or German, and that variety is a goal. Taped music is appropriate and is encouraged, along with contemporary Christian music. In each case, quality is essential.
2. Direction of Chancel Choir, Umbrella Singers, Youth Choir, with as much lay participation in the other choirs as possible. These choirs include the children's choirs, Children, Youth, and Adult Handbells, Women's and Men's Chorale, Classical Ensemble, Gospel Ensemble, and Recorder Ensemble instrumentalists.
3. Responsible for the snack supper until the kitchen is on-line.
4. Supervision including hiring and terminating of Organist, Audio Technician, and volunteer directors and accompanists.
5. Responsible for quality music at all times during the time between the worship services.
6. Other responsibilities include Adult Choir retreats/ workshops, liaison for Big Band, Music Ministry Team, serve on Worship Committee, development of new leaders, attendance at administrative board and staff meetings, teach at Laity Seminar once a year.
7. Salary for 1990 to be $_____
8. Salary increases for 1991 and 1992 to be minimum cost of living, plus merit. Further increases depend upon merit and available funds.
9. Each staff person is evaluated monthly for the first ninety days and then twice in each of the following years. It is expected that all staff persons have a clear picture of HOW to achieve the above objectives within the first ninety days.

SAMPLE WORSHIP WELCOME

We are delighted to have you worship with us at the Umbrella Church. Each Sunday, we are privileged to have many new people attending for the first time and we want you to feel welcome among us. The following information is provided for your benefit.

WE ARE THE UMBRELLA CHURCH! We have chosen the umbrella as our symbol because of the diversity of our ministry and because our family is open to all people committed to Christ. Our Mission Covenant affirms our biblical vision. "We are the people of God, called to live under the Umbrella of Love, Justice, and Mercy, to nurture the churched and win the unchurched." Again, we are glad you are here!

WE WILL SEND YOU OUR NEWSLETTER FREE! Our newsletter contains a wealth of information about the life of our church and is mailed to almost 2,000 homes each week. We will be happy to send it to you. Simply fill out the Guest Information Card located on the back of each pew. Extra copies of this week's "Under the Umbrella" are available in the Hospitality Center by the coffee pot.

SERMON TAPES ARE AVAILABLE, TOO! Audio cassette tapes of the sermons preached by our pastors are available for $3.00 per sermon. If you would like one, please fill out the order form found in today's program and place it in the offering plate, or call Esther in the church office at 349-2401.

SUNDAY SCHOOL CLASSES FOR ALL AGES! We have a Sunday school class for people of every age. Contact Shari Stephens, our Minister of Education, or Marshall B. Monroe, our Minister of Youth Ministries, or singles may contact Rev. Lynn Young for information about the classes, groups and activities in which you would like to be involved. They may all be reached through the church office at 349-2401.

WE WANT TO BE YOUR NEW FAMILY OF FAITH! We hope as you begin to feel at home in our church family that you will want to belong too! We have already made arrangements to help you do so. Simply fill out the box below and bring it forward with you as we sing the closing hymn. Our pastors will be there to welcome you. For more information on belonging, contact Rosemary Engstrom, our Minister of Evangelism, at 349-2401 and we'll help you take the first step toward belonging and becoming a part of the finest family of faith you'll ever find.

Our Staff Is Here to Help You

Ministers	Every Member of the Congregation
Pastors	Bill Easum
	John Speight, Jr.
	Lynn Young
Church Administrator	Michael Williamson
Minister of Evangelism	Rosemary Engstrom
Minister of Education	Shari Stephens
Ministers to Children	Lou Ann Knoll and Gayle Guthrie
Minister of Music	Amanda Singer
Minister of Youth	Marshall B. Monroe
Minister to Singles	Linda Colvert
Executive Assistant	Sharon Craig
Organist	Madison Pruet
Director of Preschool & Children's Day Out	Kathy Nichols
Director of Nursery & Parents' Night Out	JoGayle Kowalik
Director of Day Care	Joyce Troop
Church Secretary	Rosemary C. Maroti
Program Secretary	Sandi Pohlmann
School Secretary	Sue Summers
Audio Technician	Michael Labay
Financial Secretary	Jill Schafer
Receptionist	Esther Matera
Mission Church	Nuevo Laredo, Mexico
Church Sponsored Seminarian	Raul Garcia
Custodial Staff	Rudy Hernandez
	Carlos Sanchez

TO BELONG TO OUR CHURCH FAMILY
(present this to the pastor during final hymn)

Name(s)_____Phone_____

Address_____Zip_____

Children & Birthdays

_____ _____

You may belong by:
   Profession of Faith_____Restoration of Vows_____
   Transfer of Membership_____Baptism & Profession_____

Former Church

_____

Address_____

NOTES

Introduction: Fast Forward

1. Tex Sample, *U.S. Lifestyles and Mainline Churches* (Louisville: Westminster/John Knox Press, 1990).
2. Cheryl Russell, *100 Predictions for the Baby Boom* (New York: Plenum Press, 1987), p. 23.

II. Future-Active Leadership

1. Michael Kami, *Trigger Points* (New York: McGraw Hill, 1989), p. 43.

III. Organizing for Ministry

1. Boyce A. Bowden, "Lay Ministry; The Key to Growth," *Circuit Rider*, May 1989, p. 5.
2. Stanley Menking, "Why Do We Fail the Laity in their Ministry?" *Circuit Rider*, May 1989, p. 9.

IV. Taking Aim at the Baby Boomer

1. Church Information & Development Services, Redhill Avenue, Suite 2-200, Costa Mesa, Calif. 92626.
2. To order *American Demographics*, write: Stanley J. Menkins, Perkins School of Theology, SMU, Dallas, Tex. 75275-0133, or call (214) 692-2251.

4. "Bring a Friend Sunday" material can be acquired from The Net Results Resource Center, 5001 Avenue N, Lubbock, Tex. 79412.
5. Eddie Fox and George Morris, *Faith Sharing* (Nashville: Discipleship Resources, 1986). Dr. Billy Abraham can be reached at Perkins School of Theology, SMU, Dallas, Tex. 75275.
6. Kirk McNeill and Robert Paul, *Reaching for the Baby Boomers* (Nashville: The General Board of Discipleship of The United Methodist Church, 1989).
7. Sample, *U.S. Lifestyles and Mainline Churches.*
8. Russel, *100 Predictions for the Baby Boom.*
9. Disciple Bible Study may be secured through the Cokesbury Service Center, 201 Eighth Avenue, South, P.O. Box 801, Nashville, Tenn. 37202-0801, or call 1-800-672-1789.
   The Bethel Bible Series may be secured by writing: P.O. Box 8398, Madison, Wis. 53708-8398.
   Trinity Bible Study may be secured by writing: P.O. Box 77, El Paso, Ark. 72045.

V. Feeding the Baby Boomer

1. See chapter 4 notes, no. 9.
2. George Gallup, Jr., *The Unchurched American...10 Years Later* (Princeton, N.J.: The Princeton Religion Research Center, 1988), p. 61.
3. For an excellent discussion of the role of the individual in the coming decades, see John Naisbitt and Patricia Aburdene, *Megatrends 2000* (New York: William Morrow and Company, 1990), pp. 298ff.
4. Lyle Schaller, "Reflections on Three Decades," *Net Results,* July 1990, pp. 10-18.
5. John Naisbitt and Patricia Aburdene, *Megatrends 2000,* pp. 216-40.
6. George Gallup, Jr. *The Unchurched American...10 Years Later,* p. 48.
7. Those interested in the program can write to Stephen Ministries, 1325 Boland, St. Louis, Mo. 63117, or call (314) 645-5511.
8. For an informative article on establishing a church-wide prayer chain, see Herb Miller, "A Prayer Chain Model," *Net Results,* June 1990, pp. 8-9.
9. You may obtain a small booklet from Foundry by writing Bauman Bible Telecast, 4620 Lee Highway, Arlington, Va. 22207.
10. James K. Wagner, *Blessed To Be A Blessing* (Nashville: Upper Room Publisher, 1980).
11. Albert Edward Day, *Letters on the Healing Ministry* (Nashville: Methodist Evangelistic Materials, 1964).

VI. *Giving Is Living*

1. To learn more about "God's Guarantee," write: In Joy, 1530 Jamacha Road, Suite D, El Cajon, Calif. 92019, or call 1-800-333-6506.
2. National Evangelistic Association, 5001 Avenue N., Lubbock, Tex. 79412-2917.
3. Kennon L. Callahan, *Twelve Keys to an Effective Church* (San Francisco: Harper & Row, 1983), pp.106-16.